Third Edition

Practical Hotel Service English

호텔실무영어

백지은· 김은숙 공저

백산출판사

21세기의 관광산업은 급속한 성장을 거듭하여 국가 전략산업으로 발전하여 왔습니다. 국민소득과 여가시간의 증대로 삶의 욕구가 더욱 높아짐과 더불어 관광산업은 큰 비중을 차지하고 있습니다. 이 중에서 호텔분야의 전문 인력이 절대적으로 필요함과 동시에 국제 언어로서 영어의 중요성은 절대적으로 필요한 현실입니다. 호텔산업에서 전문 인력을 양성 배출하기 위해서는 영어실력 향상은 어느 때보다도 절실한 실정입니다.

본서 'Practical Hotel Service English'는 호텔에서 사용되는 실무영어를 중심으로 의사소통 능력의 함양을 목표로 하였습니다. 간단한 표현을 반복 연습으로 인하여 완벽하게 소화할 수 있도록 시도하였고, 호텔에서 사용되는 회화내용에 따른 Key Words를 보충 설명하였습니다. 따라서 본 교재를 통해 의사소통의 향상 및 호텔실무의 이해가 더불어 이루어지리라 생각됩니다.

이 책의 구성은 크게 객실 부문과 식음료 부문으로 영역을 분류하였습니다. 제1부 객실 부문은 제1장 객실예약 서비스Ⅰ, 제2장 객실예약 서비스Ⅱ, 제3장 교환원 서비스, 제4장 Concierge Service, 제5장 Door man/Bell man ServiceⅠ, 제6장 Door man/Bell man ServiceⅡ, 제7장 Front ServiceⅠ, 제8장 Front ServiceⅡ, 제9장 Housekeeping Service와 제2부 식음료 부문에서는 제10장 Room Service, 제11장 Food & Beverage ServiceⅠ, 제12장 Food & Beverage ServiceⅡ 및 제13장 Food & Beverage ServiceⅢ 등의 현장 중심의 운영실무 영어를 다루었습니다. 더불어 제3부 Review 부분의 제14장 ActivityⅠ 및 제15장 ActivityⅡ에서는 상황별 회화내용 쓰고 말하기를 추가하였고, 그 외 OPIc by Jenny Baek, OPIc Vocaburary, Hotel Glossary, Answer key를 부록으로 첨부하였습니다. 본서는 제1장부터 제13장까지 내용 반복 연습(Review)을 통한 실무에 활용되는 상황별 표현을 완벽하게 익힐 수 있도록 학습자 중심으로 구성하였습니다.

각 장마다 여러 상황에 따른 사례들로 연습문제를 풀 수 있게 준비하였고, 호텔영어에 대한 흥미와 자신감을 가질 수 있도록 배려하였으며, 호텔산업과 관련된 분야를 공부하는 학생뿐만 아니라 외국여행을 즐기며 호텔을 이용하는 고객들도 호텔용어를 이해하고 사용할 수 있도록 문장들로 구성하였습니다.

따라서 본 교재의 활용을 통하여 호텔경영 전공자 및 호텔산업 종사자뿐 아니라 호텔을 이용하시는 분들께도 의사소통 능력(Communication Ability)을 향상시키는 것을 최종목표로 합니다.

제2판에서 약속드렸던 수정되어야 할 부분과 오류에 대해서는 점검하여 보완·발전시켰습니다. 또한 이번 제3판에서는 읽기(Reading Comprehension)를 추가하여 통합영어교육을 완성하였습니다. 앞으로도 수정되어야 할 부분과 오류 및 부족한 부분은 계속해서 보완·발전시켜 나갈 것을 약속드립니다.

본서가 오랜 시간 좋은 책으로 기억될 수 있도록 도움을 주신 삼성전자 한국총괄 윤준호 상무님과 하영수 상무님, 주상현 부장님께 감사드립니다.

아울러 어려운 여건에도 이번 제3판의 출간을 흔쾌히 맡아주신 백산출판사의 진욱상 사장님, 진성원 상무님께 깊은 감사를 드리며, 이경희 부장님을 비롯한 직원 여러분의 노고에도 진심으로 감사드립니다.

마지막으로, 곁에서 묵묵히 지원해주신 부모님과 남동생 백창훈에게 고맙고 사랑한다는 말을 전하고 싶습니다.

저자 씀

Contents

제2부 식음료 부문

Column 1

영어적 사고를 키우는 방법

1. 영어적 사고 vs 한국적 사고 차이를 이해

둘의 차이를 극단적으로 쉽게 풀어보면, "영어와 한국어 간의 어순의 차이"로 볼 수 있다. 이런 사고의 차이는 특히 사물 또는 사람이 둘 이상 있어 그 사이에 어떤 액션이 취해질 때 드러나게 된다.

> EX1) 동일한 사고 전개(사물 또는 사람이 하나일 때)
> 나는 잠 잤어. (주어+동사) = I slept. (주어+동사)
> Ex2) 다른 사고 전개(사물 또는 사람이 하나 이상이면서 그 둘의 관계가 주체와 객체 관계를 가질 때
> 나는 그 사람을 때렸어. (주어+목적어+동사)
> ⇒ I hit the man. (주어+동사+목적어)

한국어에서는 주어와 목적어 간의 관계(상황 설정)가 먼저 나오게 되며, 나중에 그 관계 속에서 벌어진 일이 나오게 된다.

영어에서는 주어가 어떤 일을 했는지 먼저 나오며, 누구에게(목적어) 했는지가 다음에 나오게 된다.

2. 쉬운 영어 문장을 통한 기본 이해

한국어에서 "주어+목적어+동사"가 영어에서 "주어+동사+목적어"가 되는 것은 쉬운 문장을 익히면서 자연스럽게 익힐 수 있는 부분이다.

"주어+동사+목적어"의 "영어적 사고"는 비교적 간단하기에 쉬운 문장을 익히는 것만으로도 영어적 사고를 한 것이라 볼 수 있는 것이다.

EX1) I drove the car.

그런데 문제는 우리의 생각이 이렇게 항상 간단하지만은 않다는 것이다. 간단하지 않다는 것은 문장에 부연 설명이 들어간다는 것을 의미하기도 한다.

I drove the car.에서 그 차는 어제 도난당한 차였다.

두 문장으로 나누어 설명할 수 있지만, 가능한 한 빨리 동일한 의미를 전달하려는 인간의 욕구는 두 문장을 하나의 문장으로 빠르게 전달하려 노력하게 된다.

Ex2) I drove the car that was stolen yesterday.

"나는 그 차를 운전하였다"와 "그 차는 어제 도난당한 차였다"의 이 두 정보를 하나의 문장에 담았다.

마치 그 차가 어떤 차였는지 부연 설명하는 것같이 문장이 구성되었다. 하지만 여전히 문장의 가장 앞에는 I drove "내가 운전했다"는 결과가 먼저 나왔다.

이 문장을 한국어로 하면 다음과 같다.

Ex3) "나는 [어제 도난당한] 그 차를 운전했다."

한국어 문장에서는 부연 설명이 주어 다음, 설명하려는 단어 앞에 나왔다. 이런 한국어 문장에 익숙한 대부분의 한국 학습자는 기본적인 I love you(주어+동사+목적어)에서 좀 더 발전된 문장에서는 혼란을 가질 수밖에 없는 것이다.

이런 문법 사항은 이론상으로는 어렵지 않게 이해될 수 있지만, 실제 대화에서 듣고 말할 때는 바로 적용되지 않는 것이 사실이다.

결국 이 영어적 사고를 제대로 이해하고 습득하는 것이 영어 학습 성공에 중요한 역할을 하게 된다. 어떻게 해야 영어적 사고를 보다 빨리 습득할 수 있을까?

3. 영어적 사고 습득 방법으로 익숙해지기

① 영어 문장을 가능한 한 많이 접하되, 한국어식 해석을 하지 않는다.
② 리스닝 시 대부분의 영어 문장에서는 결과가 먼저 나온다는 것을 염두해 둔다.
③ 스피킹 시 결과부터 말한다는 것을 항상 염두해 둔다.
④ 같은 값이라면 한국어보다는 영어로 접하려고 노력한다.

영어 유창성 읽기의 7가지 원리(Principles)

읽기를 통한 말하기의 원리를 중심으로 유창한 스피킹을 구사할 수 있는 리딩 훈련법을 소개한다.

1. 영어 강세의 원리를 이해하자

강세를 받는 발음은 일반적으로 소리가 더 강하고, 더 높고, 더 길다. 영어의 강세와 관련하여, 강세 위치가 바꾸면 모음의 질에 변화가 생긴다. 영어의 강세 모음은 완전모음으로 발음된다. 그러나 강세를 받지 않은 모음들은 약한 모음으로 발음된다. 일반적으로 강세를 받지 않은 모음은 /어/ 나 /이/로 발음된다. 예를 들어, ball이 강세를 받으면 /볼/로 발음되지만, balloon에서처럼, ball이 강세를 받지 않으면 /벌룬/으로 발음된다. 그런데 우리의 영어학습자들은 아직도 문자 위주로 글을 보니 단어를 철자 위주로 잘못 이해하는 학습자들이 많다.

강세모음과 비강세모음 발음 비교

강세모음	비강세 모음
ball	ballon
fast	breakfast
late	chocolate
men	women
social	society
recorder	a record

한편, 영어의 복합어 강세는 첫 번째가 주강세이고 두 번째가 부강세이다.

sunrise (일출)	babysit (아이를 돌보다)
flash light (전등)	tiptoe (조심스럽게 걷다)
toy car (장난감차)	old-fashioned (구식의)
white house (백악관)	black board (칠판의)
English teacher (영어선생)	light house (등대)

한편 복합어의 경우, 강세가 바뀌면 뜻이 달라지는 경우도 많다.
예를 들면, 다음과 같은 경우이다.

White house (흰 집)	black board (검은색 판자)
English teacher (영국인 선생)	light house (밝은 집)

이처럼 영어는 강세에 따라 뜻이 바뀔 수 있으니 말하기에 있어서 발음에 주의해야
한다.

2. 명사 · 동사 · 형용사 · 부사는 강하게 읽는다

영어의 문장 강세는 일반적으로 명사 · 동사 · 형용사 · 부사와 같은 내용어는 독립적인
의미가 있고 강세를 받는다. 예를 들어, flower(명사), play(동사), happy(형용사), quietly
(부사) 등은 문장에서 강세를 받는다.

반면 기능어는 관사 · 전치사 · 접속사 · 조동사와 같이 독립적인 뜻이 없이 문장 가운
데서 앞뒤 관계를 맺어 주는 문법적 역할을 전달만 한다. 이런 것들은 강세를 안 받고
약하게 발음만 한다. 예를 들어, a/the(관사), for/in(전치사), that/and(접속사), can/will
(조동사), you/he(대명사), which/who(관계대명사) 등과 같은 단어들은 문장에서 약하게
읽는다.

다음 문장들을 큰 소리로 읽어 본다. 고딕체는 내용어로 강하게 읽고 나머지는 기능어로 약하게 읽는다. 읽는 동안에 우리는 강약의 리듬을 조금씩 느낄 수 있다.

The room was burning. (방이 타고 있었다.)
We should help poor people. (우리는 가난한 사람들을 도와야 한다.)
He had not walked since he was born. (그는 태어날 때부터 걷질 못했다.)
Buck had never seen dogs fight like these dogs.
(벽은 이 개들처럼 개들이 싸우는 것을 본 적이 없다.)

3. 문장의 마지막 명사나 동사는 강하게 읽는다

영어를 읽을 때 한 단어에 2개 이상의 내용어가 있을 때는 제일 마지막 내용에서 주요 문장 강세를 받는다. 예를 들어, 다음 2개의 문장을 보자.

Ex1) Jane bought a new car at Creeds.
(제인은 크리드에서 새 차를 샀다.)

Ex2) Did he gave her three DOLLARS for me?
(그는 그녀에게 나를 위해 3달러를 주었니?)

4. 영어는 강세에 따라 움직이는 언어이다

영어는 강세 음절과 무강세 음절이 규칙적으로 반복되어 일정한 리듬을 갖는다. 예를 들어, 다음과 같은 문장을 읽어 보자.

The boy is interested in enlarging his vocabulary.
(소년은 그의 어휘를 늘리는 데 관심이 있다.)

이 문장에서 각 부분마다 내용어(boys/interested/enlarging/vocabulary)는 강하고 길게 읽지만, 기능어(the/is /in/his)는 약하고 짧게 읽는다.

이런 원리로 영어 문장을 읽으면 아래에 나오는 6개의 문장을 읽는 데 걸리는 시간이 음절의 수와 관계없이 비슷하게 되는 것을 경험할 수 있다.

영어는 강세에 따라 리듬을 갖기 때문에 강세 음정과 무강세 음절이 규칙적으로 반복하여 일정한 리듬을 갖는다. 우리가 발음 시에 주의할 점은 영어 원어민은 음절 수와 관계없이 내용어를 중심으로 강세를 읽고, 기능어가 많이 포함되어 있더라도 전체 문장을 읽는 데 걸리는 시간이 비슷하다는 것이다.

예를 들어, 다음 문장은 각각 큰 소리로 읽어 본다.

Birds	eat	worms
The birds	eat	worms
The birds	eat	the worms
The birds	will eat	the worms
The birds	will have eaten	the worms
A	B	C

위의 문장들에서 A, B, C 부분은 내용어를 중심으로 빨리 읽고, 기능어는 약하고 축약된 소리로 발음하기 때문에 전체 문장을 읽는 시간은 거의 비슷하게 되는 것이다. 각 부분에 나오는 단어들은 음절의 수와 관계없이 거의 같은 속도로 읽어 가게 된다. 즉 강세 박자 언어에서는 강세를 받는 음절이 일정한 간격을 두고 반복되는 리듬을 탄다. 따라서 영어 문장을 읽는 데 걸리는 시간은 전체 음절 수가 아니라 강세를 받는 음절 수에 의해서 결정된다.

5. 사고 단위에 맞게 끊어 읽어라

예를 들어, 다음 문장들을 읽어 보자.

He told everyone // that she knew the answer.
(그는 모든 사람에게 그녀가 그 답을 알고 있다고 말했다.)

He told everyone that she knew // the answer.
(그는 그녀가 알고 있는 모든 사람에게 그 답을 말했다.)

이 문장들은 어디서 끊어 읽는가에 따라 의미가 달라지고 있다. 따라서 사고단위를 생각하며 끊어 읽는 연습을 하는 것이 중요하다.
각각의 사고 단위마다 고유한 톤을 넣어 읽어야 영어의 맛이 난다.

6. 소리의 높낮이를 구별하자

영어는 인토네이션 언어이다. 따라서 소리 높낮이에 따라 의미가 달라질 수 있다.
영어 문장은 2가지 유형의 인토네이션으로 나누어 읽는다.
첫째, 상승하강(Rising-falling) 인토네이션은 주요 문장 강세를 받는 음절에서 소리가 올라가서 문장이 끝날 때 내려가는 경우이다.
서술문·명령문·의문문의 인토네이션에 해당된다.
예를 들어, 다음의 문장들을 인토네이션을 넣어 큰 소리로 읽어보자.

• 서술문

I want to go to school. (나는 학교에 가고 싶다.)

• 명령문

Give him a pencil. (그에게 연필을 주어라.)

• 의문문

What do you want to play with it? (그것으로 무엇을 하고 싶니?)

　둘째, 상승(Rising) 인토네이션은 문장 강세를 받는 음절에서 말소리가 높아져서 문장이 끝날 때까지 계속 올라가는 것을 말한다.

　대체로 Yes or No로 대답하는 의문문에 쓰인다.

　예를 들어, 다음 문장들을 인토네이션을 넣어 큰 소리로 읽어 보자.

• Yes or No 의문문

Do you want to go to school? (학교에 가고 싶니?)

• 놀라움

What! The teacher arrived already? (뭐라고! 선생님이 벌써 도착했다고?)

• 호칭

How have you been, jennifer? (제니퍼, 그동안 어떻게 지냈니?)

　한편, 복합문의 인토네이션법은 두 개가 음조 단위에 따라 읽는다. 일반적으로 상승하강(Rising-falling) 억양이 주로 쓰인다. 다시 말해, 앞에 오는 절에서 인토네이션은 주요 문자 강세를 받는 단어에서 상승하다 하강한다.

예를 들어, 다음 문장들을 인토네이션을 넣어 큰 소리로 읽어 보자.

> When Mary left the building // it was raining.
> (메리가 건물을 떠났을 때, 비가 오고 있었다.)
>
> The teacher you say you met yesterday // has left the school.
> (당시 어제 만났다고 말한 선생님이 학교를 떠났다.)

After we have lunch // we'll go to the park.

부가의문문은 상대방의 대답을 기대할 때는 상승하강 인토네이션으로 말하고, 단지 몰라서 질문하는 경우는 상승 인토네이션으로 말한다.

예를 들어, 다음 문장들을 인토네이션을 넣어 큰 소리로 읽어 보자.

• 확신할 때

Jane is beautiful, isn't she? (제인은 아름답다, 그렇지?)

• 단지 물어 볼 때

Jane is beautiful, isn't she? (제인은 아름답다. 그렇지 않니?)

선택의문문 같은 문장은 앞의 말을 올리고 뒤의 말을 내린다.

Do you want some milk or coffee.

7. 연음을 통해 발성훈련을 하자

　연속적인 단어들의 발음하기는 영어를 유창하게 듣고, 말하는 데 매우 중요한 훈련이다. 원어민의 발음을 그대로 말하고 듣기가 어려운 것은 이러한 연음 훈련이 부족하기 때문이다.

　연음이란 부드럽고 쉽게 발음하기 위해 앞뒤에 오는 단어를 함께 연속하여 발음하는 것이다. 단어와 단어 사이에 연결되는 소리와 소리를 큰 소리로 발음해 보고 그 소리에 귀를 기울여 보자.

　1. 먼저, 단어 수준의 연음은 자음과 모음의 연음이다. 앞 단어가 자음으로 끝나고 다음 단어가 모음으로 시작하면 앞 단어의 마지막 자음은 뒤에 따라오는 모음에 연음되어 그 단어의 첫 음처럼 발음된다. 다음의 단어들을 큰 소리로 읽어 보자.

　　Pu/sh up, Se/t up, Sto/p it, Ge/t up

　2. 다음은 앞 단어나 음절이 자음군으로 끝나고 그다음 단어가 모음으로 시작하는 경우다. 이때 이전 자음군의 마지막 자음은 뒤에 오는 모음에 연음되어 그 단어의 첫 음처럼 발음된다.

　　fin/d out [fain daut], firs/t o/f all [fəs tə vəl], love/s it [ləv zit]

　영어 문장을 읽다보면 수많은 연음 발음 환경에 부딪히게 되는데, 그중에 다음과 같은 경우도 자주 접하게 된다. 다음과 같이, 앞뒤의 자음들이 서로 같은 자음으로 연결될 때 길게 발음된다.

　They help : paul, The birds : sing, Mary served : dinner

이렇게 영어는 다양한 소리 환경 속에서 연음을 하게 되는데, 영어 스피킹과 리스닝을 잘하기 위해 꼭 연습해야 하는 과정이다.

특히, 여러 개의 단어로 이루어진 구가 연음되어 마치 한 단어처럼 발음되는 경우가 많은데 다음의 예를 보기로 하자.

왼쪽과 오른쪽에 나오는 단어들의 발음이 마치 같은 것처럼 들리는 것을 경험할 수 있다.

마지막으로, 일상생활에서 많이 쓰이는 연음을 익혀 두어 편리하게 활용하도록 하자.

- want to ⇨ wanna

  I want to have a pen. (나는 펜을 갖고 싶다.)

- going to ⇨ gonna

  I am going to leave. (나는 떠나려고 한다.)

- got to ⇨ gotta

  I've got to leave. (나는 떠나야 했다.)

- have to ⇨ hafta

  I have to go right away. (나는 즉시 가야 한다.)

- has to ⇨ hasta

  She has to tell me about it. (그녀는 그것에 대해 나에게 말해야 한다.)

- ought to ⇨ oughta

  She ought to try. (그녀는 시도해야 한다.)

영어의 리딩은 위의 발음의 일반적 규칙을 토대로 반복하며 읽음으로써 영어 원어민의 소리를 익히면 유창한 영어를 구사할 수 있다. 보통 쉐도우 스피킹(shadow speaking)이 영어 스피킹 훈련의 좋은 방법이 되는데, 쉐도우 스피킹이란 원어민이 말하는 소리를 들으며 그림자처럼 따라 말하는 말하기 기법을 말한다. 이 쉐도우 스피킹은 청취력 향상과 유창한 스피킹 능력을 키우는 데 매우 도움이 된다.

제**1**부

객실 부문

Reservation Service Ⅰ
객실예약의 서비스

Reservation Service I

객실예약의 서비스

R (Reservation) : 객실예약 직원 | **G** (Guest) : 고객

Conversation 1 **Reservation, Lee bona speaking**

R Good morning. Reservation, Lee bona speaking.
How may I help you?

G Yes, I'd like to make a reservation.

R Thank you, sir. When would you like to stay with us?

G The ninth of December.

R That was December ninth for one night?

G That's right.

R Certainly, sir.
Would you mind waiting for a moment, please?
I will check available for that date.

Key Words

- Sir : 호텔 등에서 이름을 모르는 남자에 대한 경칭으로 씀
- Available Room : 호텔이 당일 판매 가능한 객실을 말하며 즉, House use, Repair 객실 등을 제외한 객실 수를 말한다.

Conversation 1 예약담당 이보나입니다.

R   안녕하십니까.
     예약담당의 이보나입니다. 무엇을 도와드릴까요?

G   네, 예약을 하고 싶습니다.

R   네, 고객님. 언제쯤 예약을 원하십니까?

G   12월 9일에 원합니다.

R   12월 9일로 1박이십니까?

G   네, 맞습니다.

R   감사합니다, 고객님. 잠시만 기다려 주시겠습니까?
     그날 예약이 가능한지 확인해 드리겠습니다.

Point Expressions

• Stay Over : 고객이 Check Out 예정 일정보다 체류기간을 적어도 1박 이상 연장하는
  것을 말한다.

• That's right : 네, 맞습니다.

Conversation 2 **How many guests will there be?**

R   Thank you for waiting, sir.

      We have several types of rooms available on that day.

      How many guests will there be?

G   Just one.

R   In that case, we would recommend a standard double room.

G   How much is it?

R   The rate is Three hundred ninety six thousand one hundred won per night, including service charge and taxes.

G   All right, I'll take it.

R   Certainly, sir. May I ask the name of the guest?

G   It's going to be for myself. James Trump is my name.

R   Thank you very much, Mr. Trump.

Key Words

• Guest : 등록된 고객, 즉 투숙고객

• Standard double room : 2인용 객실로 2인용 커다란 침대가 1개 있다.

Conversation 2 **몇 분이 투숙하실 예정이십니까?**

R 기다려 주셔서 감사합니다.

   저희는 여러 종류의 룸이 있으며 당일 예약이 가능하십니다.

   몇 분이 투숙하실 예정이십니까?

G 혼자 투숙 예정입니다.

R 혼자 투숙하신다면, 스탠다드 더블룸을 추천해 드립니다.

G 숙박료가 어느 정도 됩니까?

R 세금, 봉사료 포함해서 396,100원입니다.

G 좋습니다. 예약하겠습니다.

R 알겠습니다, 고객님. 고객님의 성함을 알려주시겠습니까?

G James Trump.

R 감사합니다, Trump 고객님.

Point Expressions

• Recommend : 호텔에서 예약을 받을 때 고객에게 객실을 추천하는 것을 말한다.

Conversation 3 Would you spell your full name, please?

R Excuse me, sir.

Would you spell your name, please?

G J-A-M-E-S for my first name and T-R-U-M-P for my family name.

R Thank you very much, sir.

May I have your telephone number, please?

G Yes, it's zero-two, three-one-four, five-seven-six-eight.

R Zero-two, three-one-four, five-seven-six-eight, is that correct?

And this is your home number, sir?

G That's right.

R Certainly, we will reserve a non-smoking room for you.

 **Key Words**

• Full name : 성명
• Non-smoking room : 비 흡연층에 위치한 객실

Conversation 3　고객님 성함의 스펠링 부탁드립니다.

R　실례합니다, 고객님. 고객님 성함의 스펠링 부탁합니다.

G　이름은 J-A-M-E-S이고, 성은 T-R-U-M-P입니다.

R　감사합니다. 고객님의 연락처를 알려주시겠습니까?

G　네, 02-314-5768입니다.

R　02-314-5768, 번호가 맞습니까. 고객님?
　　이 번호는 고객님의 집 번호입니까?

G　네, 맞습니다.

R　알겠습니다, 고객님. 금연층으로 예약해 드리겠습니다.

Point Expressions

- Is that correct? : 맞습니까?
- Prefer A or B : A와 B 중 어느 쪽을 원하십니까?

Conversation 4 **What time would you like to check-in?**

R What time would you like to check-in?

G What is your check-in time?

R Our check-in time is Two p.m.

G I see.....,

I will arrive at your hotel around Five p.m.

R Certainly, sir. Are you driving to our hotel?

G Yes, I am. Do you have parking?

R Yes, we have parking available in the basement.

Our guests can use it anytime.

G That's great.

 Key Words

- Check-in : 체크인, 고객이 호텔에 처음 도착하여 입숙절차(rooming procedure) 과정을 마치고 객실에 투숙하는 것을 말한다.
- Check-in time : 체크인 타임, 일반적인 시간은 오후 5~7시 사이가 체크인 시간이다.
- Parking : 주차

Conversation 4 몇 시에 체크인 원하십니까?

R 몇 시에 체크인 원하십니까?

G 몇 시에 체크인 가능합니까?

R 체크인 시간은 오후 2시입니다.

G 그렇군요... 한 5시 경에 도착할 예정입니다.

R 잘 알겠습니다, 고객님. 저희 호텔까지 운전하고 오십니까?

G 네. 주차가 가능합니까?

R 네, 지하에 주차장이 있습니다. 저희 호텔 투숙객께서는 아무 때나 이용하실 수 있습니다.

G 좋군요.

Point Expressions

- Are you driving to ~ : 운전하고 오십니까?
- That's great : 좋군요.

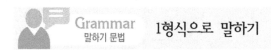

1형식으로 말하기

〈직장〉 주제와 관련하여 '당신이 다니는 직장에 대해 이야기해 주세요?' 라는 문제에 답할 때, '저는 글로벌대학교에 다닙니다.' 라고 답할 수 있어요. 이를 영어로 표현하면 다음과 같아요.

I go to Global University.

'주어가 (~에/~와) -하다'를 표현할 때는 위의 예문처럼 **[주어 + 동사 + 전치사구 /부사구]**의 1형식 문장으로 말해요. 1형식 문장에서 자주 사용하는 동사에는 go(가다), live(살다), work(일하다), walk(걷다), happen(일어나다) 등이 있어요.

I   go   to   Global   University.   [1형식 문장]
주어   동사 전치사구

• **문장 말해보기** •

1. 저는 강아지와 삽니다.
⇒ I live with my puppy.

2. 저희 어머니는 호텔에서 일하십니다.
⇒ My mother works for the Hotel.

3. 그 택시는 호텔에 도착했다.
⇒ The taxi arrived at the hotel.

 Quiz

Q. 괄호 안의 표현을 사용하여 다음의 우리말 문장을 영어로 말해보세요.

1. 제 친구는 영어 강사로 일합니다. (as an English instructor)

⇒

2. 저는 빌라에서 삽니다. (in a villa)

⇒

3. 사람들이 호수를 따라 걷습니다. (along the lake)

⇒

4. 그 일은 1년 전에 일어났습니다. (one year ago)

⇒

Practical Point

Q. 괄호 안에 알맞은 말을 넣어 말해보세요.

1.

G   Yes, I am. Do you have parking?

R   Yes, we have (   ) available in the basement. Our guests can use it anytime.

2.

R   Thank you, sir. When would you like to (   ) with us?

G   The ninth of December.

Reading Comprehension

1.

Q   How many guests will there be?

A _____

 _____

2.

Q   What is James's telephone number?

A _____

 _____

Reservation Service Ⅱ
객실예약의 서비스

Chapter 2 Reservation Service II
객실예약의 서비스

R (Reservation) : 객실예약 직원 | G (Guest) : 고객

Conversation 1   **How would you like to secure your room?**

R   How would you like to secure your room?

G   By credit card.

R   Certainly, sir. I would like to confirm your reservation.
One person for a standard double room for the night of
December ninth. Is that correct?

G   That's correct.

R   The room rate is three hundred ninety six thousand one
hundred won including service charge and taxes.

G   I understand.

R   Please feel free to contact us at any time if any changes need
to be made.

G   I will.

R   Thank you very much, My name is Lee bona.
We will be expecting you soon.
Thank you for calling, Mr. Trump.

Key Words

• Standard twin : 2인용 객실로 1인용 침대가 2개 있다.

Conversation 1   지불은 어떻게 하시겠습니까?

R   지불은 어떻게 하시겠습니까?

G   신용카드로 하겠습니다.

R   알겠습니다, 고객님. 예약 확인해 드리겠습니다.
한 분이시고, 스탠다드 더블룸으로 12월 9일 1박 맞으십니까?

G   맞습니다.

R   숙박료는 세금, 봉사료 포함해서 396,100원입니다.

G   잘 알겠습니다.

R   변경사항이 있으시면 언제든지 편하게 연락 주시기 바랍니다.

G   그렇게 하죠.

R   대단히 감사합니다. 저는 이보나입니다.
곧 만나 뵙길 기대하겠습니다. 전화 주셔서 감사합니다.
Trump 고객님.

Point Expressions

• Secure your room? : 객실을 지불하는 방법을 물을 때 쓴다.

• to Confirm : 확인해 드리다.

• Feel free to contact : 편하게 연락 주시기 바랍니다.

Conversation 2 **I'd like to cancel my reservation.**

G   My name is James Trump.

      I'd like to cancel my reservation for next Monday.

R   Certainly, Sir. I will check.

      Please hold while I locate your reservation.

G   Okay.

R   Mr. James Trump, reservation from the ninth of December for one night.

      I will take care of that, sir.

G   Is there any cancellation charge?

R   No. Our cancellation policy is twenty-four hours prior to the arrival.

G   That's great.

Key Words

• Cancellation : 고객이 사용하기로 예약한 호텔 객실에 대하여 고객의 요구에 의하여 사전에 취소되는 것을 말한다.

• Cancellation Charge : 예약되었던 내용에 대하여 어떤 이유로 인하여 취소할 경우 지불해야 하는 예약 취소 수수료를 말한다.

Conversation 2 예약을 취소하고 싶습니다만…

G 제 이름은 James Trump입니다.
다음 주 월요일 예약 건을 취소하고 싶습니다.

R 알겠습니다, 고객님. 확인해 보겠습니다.
고객님의 예약 건을 찾을 동안 잠시만 기다려 주시겠습니까?

G 알겠습니다.

R 고객님 성함은 James Trump이시고, 12월 9일 1박으로 예약하셨습니다.
제가 변경해 드리겠습니다, 고객님.

G 취소 금액이 있습니까?

R 아니요, 없습니다. 취소 금액은 도착하시는 날 하루(24시간) 전부터 받고 있습니다.

G 다행이군요.

📞 **Point Expressions**

• Cancel Reservation : 예약 건을 취소하다.

• Locate your reservation : 고객님의 예약 건을 찾다.

• Prior to the arrival : 도착하시는 날 하루 전

Conversation 3 **I'd like to change my reservation...**

G   I'd like to change my reservation.

R   Certainly, sir.

First, may I have your name please, sir?

G   My name is George Green.

R   Thank you very much, Mr. Green.

How may I help you?

G   I'd like to change my arrival date from the fifteenth to the seventeenth of May.

R   Certainly. You will be arriving on the seventeenth of May and departing on the twentieth of May as in the original reservation, is this correct?

G   That's correct.

R   I will change our reservation starting from the seventeenth of May for three nights.

Key Words

• Original reservation : 기존 예약

• Arrival date : 체크인하는 날짜

Conversation 3 예약 변경을 하고 싶습니다만…

G 예약 변경을 하고 싶습니다.

R 예. 고객님.
먼저 고객님 성함을 알려 주시겠습니까?

G 내 이름은 George Green입니다.

R 감사합니다, Green 고객님.
어떻게 도와 드릴까요?

G 체크인을 5월 15일에서 17일로 변경하고 싶습니다.

R 알겠습니다. 체크인은 17일이시고 체크아웃은 기존에 예약하신대로 20일이 맞으십니까?

G 네, 맞습니다.

R 17일 체크인하셔서 3일 투숙하시는 것으로 변경해 놓겠습니다.

Point Expressions

● Change reservation : 예약 변경

● Arriving : 호텔에 체크인하다.

● Departing : 호텔에서 체크아웃하다.

Grammar
말하기 문법

2형식으로 말하기

〈장소〉 주제와 관련해서 '당신이 투숙하는 방에 대해 이야기해 주세요?' 라는 문제에 답할 때, '제 방은 큽니다.' 라고 답할 수 있어요. 이를 영어로 표현하면 다음과 같아요.

My room is large.

'주어는 (어떠)하다/(무엇)이다'를 표현할 때는 위의 예문처럼 [주어 + 동사 + 주격보어]의 2형식 문장으로 말해요. 2형식 문장에서 자주 사용되는 동사에는 be(~하다/~이다), become(~되다), feel(~라고 느끼다) 등이 있어요.

<u>My room</u>   <u>is</u>   <u>large.</u>   [2형식 문장]
주어   동사   주격보어

• 문장 말해보기 •

1. 제 업무는 재미있습니다.
⇒ My work is interesting.

2. 그 호텔은 붐볐습니다.
⇒ The hotel was crowded.

3. 그녀는 호텔리어가 되었다.
⇒ She became a hotelier.

 Quiz

Q. 괄호 안의 표현을 사용하여 다음의 우리말 문장을 영어로 말해보세요.

1. 저희 아파트단지는 따분합니다. (my apartment complex, boring)

⇒

2. 텔레비전을 보는 동안, 저는 슬펐습니다. (I, sad)

⇒

3. 저는 편안해졌습니다. (I, comfortable)

⇒

4. 그는 약간 긴장했습니다. (He, a little nervous)

⇒

Practical Point

Q. 괄호 안에 알맞은 말을 넣어 말해보세요.

1.

    o Ms, we are sorry but the line seems to be (   ) at the moment.

    G Very well, I'll call back later.

2.

    G Is there any (   )?

    R No. Our cancellation policy is twenty-four hours prior to the arrival.

Reading Comprehension

1.

Q How kinds of room does Mr. trump make reservation?

A _____

_____

2.

Q When does Mr.Green want to make reservation?

A _____

_____

Operator's Service
교환원의 서비스

- **Conversation 1** : Thank you for calling the Global Hotel.
- **Conversation 2** : I will connect you now.
- **Conversation 3** : Do you speak English or Korean?
- **Conversation 4** : I'm very sorry but the line is busy.
- **Conversation 5** : I beg your pardon?
- **Grammar**(말하기 문법) : 3형식으로 말하기
- **Quiz**
- **Practical Point**
- **Reading Comprehension**

Chapter 3
Operator's Service
교환원의 서비스

O (Operator) : 교환원 | G (Guest) : 고객

Conversation 1 **Thank you for calling the Global Hotel.**

O Thank you for calling the Global Hotel.
   This is Lee bona speaking, may I help you?

G Good morning, I'd like to make a Reservations.

O Yes, sir.
   I will connect you to Reservations.
   One moment, please.

G Thank you for your waiting.

O You're welcome.

 Key Words

- Outside Call (아웃사이드 콜) : 외부전화, 즉 호텔 외부로부터 전화교환대에 들어오는 전화를 말한다.
- Operator (전화교환) : 호텔 내의 전화교환 부서이다.

Conversation 1 전화주셔서 감사합니다. **Global** 호텔입니다.

O   안녕하십니까? Global 호텔의 이소라입니다.
    무엇을 도와 드릴까요?

G   안녕하세요? 예약을 하고 싶습니다.

O   네, 고객님.
    예약과로 연결해 드리겠습니다. 잠시만 기다려 주십시오.

G   기다려주셔서 감사합니다.

O   감사합니다.

 Point Expressions

• Hold on : 기다리다.

• Connect to : 연결하다.

Conversation 2   **I will connect you now.**

○   Ms, we are sorry but the line seems to be busy at the moment.

ᴳ   Very well, I'll call back later.

○   Thank you for your understand.

ᴳ   You're welcome.

○   Oh, hold on, please.

ᴳ   Yes, what did you say?

○   The line is open. I will connect you now.

   Key Words

● Domestic Call(도메스틱 콜) : 시내, 시외전화
● Ms(미즈) : 여성 고객의 신분을 모를 경우 넌지시 알리기 위해 사용하는 경어로서 미스
   (Miss)와 미세스(Mrs)를 합친 여성의 경칭이다.

Conversation 2 바로 연결해 드리겠습니다.

○ 고객님, 죄송합니다만 지금 통화 중입니다.

G 괜찮습니다. 다시 전화하죠.

○ 대단히 감사합니다.

G 천만에요.

○ 잠시만요, 고객님.

G 네, 왜요?

○ 통화가 끝났습니다. 지금 바로 연결해 드리겠습니다.

📞 **Point Expressions**

• The line is busy : 통화 중입니다.

• The line is open : 통화가 끝났습니다.

Conversation 3 **Do you speak English or Korean?**

○ Good morning, thank you for calling the Global Hotel.
This is Joo sanghyun speaking. How May I help you?

ⓖ Jo reggelt Kivanok! Hogy van?
Bocsanat, beszel magyarul?

○ Excuse me, could you repeat that, please?

ⓖ Bocsanat, beszel magyarul? Hungarian language...

○ Excuse me, but I'm afraid there is no Hungarian speaking
staff available.
Do you speak English or Korean?

ⓖ Nem... koszonom szepen (hung up)

 Key Words

• ISD(International Subscriber Dialing) : 국제 다이얼 통화로 전화를 거는 방법은 다
음과 같다.

(International Code + Nationality Code + Area code + Telephone No)

• Telephone Traffic Sheet(텔레폰 트래픽시트) : 통화 수와 장거리 요금을 기록한 통화량
기록명세서를 말한다.

Conversation 3 영어나 한국어가 가능하십니까?

○ 안녕하십니까. Global 호텔의 주상현입니다.
무엇을 도와 드릴까요?

G Jo reggelt kivanok! Hogy van?
Bocsanat, beszel magyarul?

○ 죄송합니다. 다시 말씀해 주시겠습니까?

G Bocsanat, beszel magyarul? Hungarian Inguage...

○ 죄송합니다만, 헝가리어를 할 수 있는 직원이 없습니다.
영어나 한국어가 가능하십니까?

G Nem... koszonom szepen (전화 끊어짐)

 Point Expressions

• Repeat : 다시 말하다.

• I'm afraid : 죄송합니다만

• available : 있습니다.

Conversation 4 I'm very sorry but the line is busy.

ᴳ I'd like to speak to your concierge.

ᴼ Certainly. One moment, please.

ᴼ I'm very sorry but the line is busy.

ᴳ All right, then, could you ask your concierge to call me back?

ᴼ Certainly. May I have your telephone number starting with the country code?

ᴳ Sure. I'm calling from San Francisco, 1 as the national code and 415 as the city code for San Francisco...

 Key Words

• Concierge : 컨시어지는 프랑스의 위그 카페 시대에서 루이 11세 시대 사이에 궁궐 안에 살면서 다양한 권리와 특권을 누리고, 궁전의 일정한 지역 내의 사법권을 행사하며 왕의 저택을 관리하던 공무원이었음.
현대에는 호텔 내에서 일정의 Door Keeper의 의미로 벨 서비스라고도 하며, 호텔에 관한 정보나 호텔 외부의 레스토랑, 관광 정보, 극장, 교통편 등의 각종 안내를 담당하는 등의 포괄적인 서비스를 제공하는 일종의 안내인이라고 할 수 있다.

Conversation 4 죄송합니다만, 통화중입니다.

G   컨시어지와 통화하고 싶습니다. 연결해 주시겠습니까?

O   물론입니다. 잠시만 기다려 주십시오.

O   죄송합니다만, 통화중입니다.

G   그러면 컨시어지에 전화 부탁한다고 전해 주시겠습니까?

O   네, 고객님.
    고객님의 전화번호를 국가번호부터 알려 주시겠습니까?

G   네, 저는 미국 샌프란시스코에서 전화하고 있습니다.
    미국의 국가번호는 1이고 415는 샌프란시스코의 지역번호입니다.

Point Expressions

• Certainly : 물론입니다.

• Call me back : 전화를 부탁하다.

Conversation 5 **I beg your pardon?**

ⓖ Hi, My name is Christiana, I am calling from Rome, Italy.

ⓞ Yes, Ms. Christiana.

ⓖ I would like to talk to one of your guest.

ⓞ Yes, Miss. Christiana, may I have the guest's name, please?

ⓖ Yes, her name is Powell.

ⓞ I beg your pardon?

ⓖ Clara, Ms Clara Powell.

ⓞ Could you please spell her last name?

ⓖ Yes, P-O-W-E-L-L, Powell.
    She said she would be arriving on Monday.

ⓞ Thank you. I have located her. I will connect you.

Key Words

• Spell : 스펠링
• Last name : 이름 중 성씨를 의미한다.

Conversation 5 (죄송합니다만) 다시 한 번 말씀해 주시겠습니까?

G 안녕하세요. 이태리 로마에서 전화하는 Christiana라고 합니다.

O 네, Christiana 고객님.

G 그곳에 투숙 중인 고객과 통화하고 싶은데요.

O 네, Christiana 고객님.
찾으시는 고객님의 성함을 알려 주시겠습니까?

G 네, 그녀의 이름은 Powell입니다.

O 죄송합니다. 다시 한 번 말씀해 주시겠습니까?

G Clara, Ms. Clara Powell입니다.

O 찾으시는 고객님 성함의 스펠링을 부탁합니다.

G 네, P-O-W-E-L-L, Powell입니다.
월요일에 도착한다고 했습니다.

O 감사합니다. 찾으시는 고객님이 계십니다.
지금 연결해 드리겠습니다.

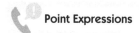

Point Expressions

• Beg your pardon? : 죄송합니다만, 다시 한 번 말씀해 주시겠습니까?

Grammar
말하기 문법   **3형식으로 말하기**

〈여행〉 주제와 관련하여 '좋아하는 여행지는 어디입니까?' 라는 질문에 답할 때, '저는 궁을 좋아합니다.' 라고 답할 수 있어요. 이를 영어로 표현하면 다음과 같아요.

I like palaces.

'주어가 ~을 -하다'를 표현할 때는 위의 예문처럼 [주어 + 동사 + 목적어]의 3형식 문장으로 말해요. 3형식 문장에서 자주 사용하는 동사에는 have(~을 가지다), like(~을 좋아하다), play((운동)을 하다/(악기)를 연주하다), watch(~을 보다), use(~을 사용하다), discuss(~을 논의하다) 등이 있어요.

I   like   palaces.   [3형식 문장]
주어   동사   목적어

• 문장 말해보기 •

1. 그는 호화스런 차를 가지고 있습니다.

⇒ He has a gorgeous car.

2. 저는 드라마를 봅니다.

⇒ I watch dramas.

 Quiz

Q. 괄호 안의 표현을 사용하여 다음의 우리말 문장을 영어로 말해보세요.

1. 저는 제 친구들과 야구를 합니다. (baseball, with my friends)

   ⇒

2. 저는 노트북 컴퓨터를 가지고 있습니다. (a notebook computer)

   ⇒

3. 저는 바닥을 쓸기 위해서 진공청소기를 사용합니다.

   (a vacuum cleaner, to sweep the floor)

   ⇒

4. 저는 재즈 음악을 좋아합니다. (jazz music)

   ⇒

Practical Point

Q. 괄호 안에 알맞은 말을 넣어 말해보세요.

1.

G Yes, her name is Powell.

O I beg your (   )?

2.

O Excuse me, but I'm afraid there is no Hungarian speaking

staff (   ).

Do you speak English or Korean?

G Nem... koszonom szepen (hung up)

Reading Comprehension

1.

Q   What is the name of the Hotel?

A   _____

   _____

2.

Q   Has She connected to Domestic call?

A   _____

   _____

3.

Q   Where does the guest call to?

A   _____

   _____

Chapter 4

Concierge Service
컨시어지 서비스

Chapter 4

Concierge Service
컨시어지 서비스

C (Concierge) : 컨시어지 직원 | G (Guest) : 고객

Conversation 1 **Can you arrange a car with driver for me?**

> G Can you arrange a car with driver for me?
>
> C Certainly, sir.
>   What is your destination and when do you need to arrive?
>
> G I have a meeting at nine tomorrow morning at Yeoui-do.
>   How long does it take from here to Yeoui-do?
>
> C It takes approximately thirty minutes.
>
> G Well, I can leave here at eight thirty, can't I?
>
> C Considering the heavy traffic, I suggest that you leave here
>   earlier in order to insure that you get there on time.
>
> G I see.
>
> C The car will be ready at eight fifteen, so you can come down
>   to the main entrance when you are ready.

Key Words

• Destination : 관광지

 **Conversation 1** 차량과 기사를 준비해 주시겠습니까?

G 차량과 기사를 준비해 주시겠습니까?

C 알겠습니다, 고객님.
원하시는 목적지와 도착시간은 어떻게 되십니까?

G 내일 오전 9시에 여의도에서 미팅이 있습니다.
여기서 여의도까지 얼마나 걸립니까?

C 대략 30분 정도 소요됩니다.

G 그럼, 여기서 8시 30분에 떠나야겠죠?

C 교통 체증을 감안하신다면, 여기서 좀 일찍 출발하셔야 약속시간에 맞춰서 도착하실 수
있을 것 같습니다.

G 알겠습니다.

C 내일 아침 8시 15분에 정문에 나오시면 차량이 대기하고 있을 겁니다.

 Point Expressions

• Arrange a car : 차량을 대기하다.

Conversation 2   **Do you have any recommendations for sightseeing?**

G   Do you have any recommendations for sightseeing?

C   Yes. Is this your first visit to Korea, madam?

G   No, I come to Korea every year. Unfortunately, there is never enough time for sightseeing.
This trip, I'm very lucky, I'm free for a whole day today.

C   That is great. We are pleased to recommend many places for you.
First of all, are there any places that you would like to visit?

G   Well, I don't know anything about Korea even though I've visited several times.
Please show me a couple of good places that could be seen in a day.

C   Certainly, madam.
Would you like to join an organized tour or go on your own?

G   I prefer to go around on my own.

   **Key Words**

• Recommendations : 추천
• sightseeing : 관광

Conversation 2   추천해 줄 만한 관광지가 있습니까?

G   추천해 줄 만한 관광지가 있습니까?

C   네, 고객님. 한국은 처음 방문하신 겁니까?

G   아니요. 해마다 한국에 옵니다.
    아쉽게도 관광할 시간이 충분하지 않았습니다.
    운 좋게도 오늘은 여행할 시간이 있습니다.

C   잘 됐습니다. 저희가 많은 곳을 추천해 드리겠습니다.
    먼저 특별히 가보고 싶으신 곳이 있으십니까?

G   아니요, 몇 번 방문했지만 서울에 대해선 아무 것도 모릅니다.
    하루 일정으로 둘러볼 수 있는 관광지를 몇 군데 추천해 주세요.

C   알겠습니다. 고객님.
    관광으로 가시겠습니까, 아니면 혼자 둘러보시겠습니까?

G   혼자 둘러보는 게 좋습니다.

Point Expressions

• Join an organized tour : 관광으로 가다.

• go on your own : 혼자 둘러보다.

Conversation 3 **We recommend Gyeongbokgung Palace and Deoksugung Palace.**

c   We recommend Gyeongbokgung Palace and Deoksugung Palace for a one day sightseeing trip.
    Both are one of Korea's representative palaces in Seoul, famous for its magnificent structure and unique beauty.

G   I've heard of both of them.
    Will it be most convenient to travel by taxi?

c   Yes, we suggest that you take the taxi for Gyeongbokgung Palace.
    You can walk for Deoksugung Palace, which takes only 10 minutes.
    Have a pleasant day, madam/sir.

Key Words

• One day sightseeing trip : 1일 코스의 관광
• Representative place : 대표적인 장소

Conversation 3 경복궁과 덕수궁을 추천합니다.

C 1일 코스의 관광을 안내해 드리겠습니다.

경복궁과 덕수궁을 추천해 드립니다.

경복궁과 덕수궁은 한국의 대표적인 궁들로, 멋진 구조물과 독특한 아름다움으로 유명합니다.

G 이 두 곳에 대해서 들은 적이 있습니다.

택시로 이동하는 것이 가장 편리할까요?

C 경복궁은 택시로 이동하실 것을 권해 드립니다.

덕수궁은 걸으시면 약 10분 정도 소요됩니다.

즐거운 시간되시길 바랍니다.

 Point Expressions

- Famous for : ~로 유명한
- Have a pleasant day : 즐거운 시간되시길 바랍니다.

Conversation 4 **I'd like to buy some Korean souvenirs...**

G   I'd like to buy some Korean souvenirs for my wife.

C   What kind of items are you looking for?

G   Something typically Korean...
    Well, I'm not sure what to get.

C   There are souvenir shops in a Korean traditional street called
    Insadong.
    You can see many examples of Korean crafts and china.
    We believe you can find something that you like there.

G   That sounds good. Can you tell me how to get there?

C   Yes, The best way would be taking a taxi.
    It takes about 10 minutes.

Key Words

• Souvenirs : 기념품

Conversation 4 한국식 기념품을 사고 싶은데요…

G 아내에게 줄 한국식 기념품을 사고 싶은데요.

C 어떤 종류의 기념품을 찾으십니까, 고객님?

G 무언가 전형적인 한국의…
   잘 모르겠는데요.

C 인사동이라는 한국 전통 문화의 거리에 기념품 가게가 있습니다.
   그곳에 가시면 많은 한국 공예품과 도자기를 보실 수 있습니다.
   그곳에서 고객님이 원하시는 무언가를 찾으실 수 있을 겁니다.

G 좋습니다. 어떻게 가야 하나요?

C 네, 고객님. 택시를 이용하실 것을 권해 드립니다.
   약 10분 정도 걸립니다.

 **Point Expressions**

● Can you tell me how to get there : 어떻게 가야 하나요?

Conversation 5   **How can I get to Incheon Airport?**

G   How can I get to Incheon Airport?

C   There is a limousine bus and taxis. Also, we can arrange a
car with driver.

G   I see. Which way is the quickest?

C   Of course, by taxi or a car with driver.
It takes approximately one hour and fifteen minutes.
However, it will be quite expensive.

G   How much is it?

C   Sixty thousand won by taxi, one hundred thousand one for
a car with driver.

G   Too expensive! I can't believe it!
How about the limousine bus?

C   It's fourteen thousand won.
It takes approximately one hour and a half.

G   Well. I'll take the limousine bus.

Key Words

• Limousine : 리무진

Conversation 5 인천 공항은 어떻게 갑니까?

G 인천 공항은 어떻게 갑니까?

C 리무진 버스와 택시가 있습니다.
   또한 저희 기사가 운전하는 렌터카 예약도 가능합니다.

G 알겠습니다. 어떤 것이 가장 빠릅니까?

C 물론 택시와 렌터카가 빠릅니다. 대략 1시간 15분 정도 걸립니다.
   그렇지만 요금이 비쌉니다.

G 얼마입니까?

C 택시로는 약 60,000원이고, 기사가 운전하는 차로는 약 100,000원입니다.

G 너무 비싸네요.

C 리무진 버스는 어떻습니까?
   14,000원에 대략 1시간 반 걸립니다.

G 리무진 버스를 이용해야 할 것 같군요.

 Point Expressions

• Which way is the quickest? : 어떤 것이 가장 빠릅니까?

• Arrange a car with driver : 기사가 운전하는 차를 예약하다.

4형식으로 말하기

〈업무〉 주제와 관련하여 '누가 팩스 보내는 법을 알려주었나요?' 라는 문제에 답할 때, '상사께서 저희에게 방법을 가르쳐 주셨어요.' 라고 답할 수 있어요. 이를 영어로 표현하면 다음과 같아요.

Our boss taught us thc way.

'주어가 ~에게 …을 -하다'를 표현할 때는 위의 예문처럼 [주어 + 동사 + 간접목적어 + 직접목적어]의 4형식 문장으로 말해요. 4형식 문장에서 자주 사용되는 동사에는 give(~에게 …을 주다), buy(~에게 …을 사주다), show(~에게 …을 보여주다), teach(~에게 …을 가르쳐 주다) 등이 있어요.

Our boss	taught	us	the way.	[4형식 문장]
주어	동사	간접목적어	직접목적어	

• 문장 말해보기 •

1. 제 선생님께서 제게 특별 과제를 주었습니다.

⇒ My teacher gave me a special assignment.

2. 저의 부모님께서 제게 책상을 사주셨습니다.

⇒ My parents bought me a desk.

 Quiz

Q. 괄호 안의 표현을 사용하여 다음의 우리말 문장을 영어로 말해보세요.

1. 그가 우리에게 야구 하는 법을 보여주었습니다. (how to play baseball)

⇒

2. 저는 저희 선생님께 선물을 사주었습니다. (My teacher, some gifts)

⇒

3. 저희 친구가 스마트폰 사용 방법을 가르쳐 주었습니다.

(my friend, how to use the smart phone)

⇒

4. 제 친구가 제게 책을 주었습니다. (My friend, a book)

⇒

Practical Point

Q. 괄호 안에 알맞은 말을 넣어 말해보세요.

1.

   G   How can I get to Incheon Airport?

   C   There is a (   ) bus and taxis. Also, we can arrange a car with driver.

2.

   G   I'd like to buy some Korean (   ) for my wife.

   C   What kind of items are you looking for?

3.

   C   We recommend Gyeongbokgung Palace and Deoksugung Palace for a one day (   ).
Both are one of Korea's representative palaces in Seoul, famous for its magnificent structure and unique beauty.

   G   I've heard of both of them.
Will it be most convenient to travel by taxi?

Reading Comprehension

1.

Q How long does it take to Yeoui-do?

A _____

_____

2.

Q Does the guest want to join an organized tour?

A _____

_____

Chapter 5

Door man/Bell man Service I

도어맨/벨맨 서비스

Chapter 5

Door man/Bell man Service I
도어맨/벨맨 서비스

D (Door man) : 도어맨 | **B** (Bell man) : 벨맨 | **G** (Guest) : 고객

Conversation 1 **Welcome.**

D   Welcome to the Global Hotel.
    Are you checking in, sir?

G   Yes.

D   May I help with your luggage, sir?

G   Yes, thanks.

D   Are there any other pieces?

G   No, that's all.

D   May I have your name, please?

G   My name is Ford.

D   May I ask your full name, sir?

G   David Ford.

D   Thank you very much, Mr. Ford.
    I will take you to the Front Desk.
    This way, please.

 Key Words

• Luggage : 수하물, 고객의 짐

Conversation 1 어서 오십시오.

D 어서 오십시오. 글로벌 호텔입니다.
   체크인하십니까, 고객님?

G 네.

D 짐을 들어 드리겠습니다, 고객님.

G 네, 감사합니다.

D 다른 짐은 없으십니까?

G 없습니다. 이게 전부입니다.

D 고객님, 성함이 어떻게 되십니까?

G Ford입니다.

D 고객님의 풀네임(full name)을 알 수 있을까요?

G David Ford입니다.

D 대단히 감사합니다, Ford 고객님.
   프런트로 안내해 드리겠습니다. 이쪽으로 오십시오.

Point Expressions

● Welcome : 어서 오십시오.

● May I ask your full name, sir? : 고객님의 존함을 알 수 있을까요?

● This way, please : 이쪽으로 오십시오.

Conversation 2 **I will show you to your room.**

B   I will show you to your room, Mr. Ford.
     Elevators are on your right.
     This way, please.

B   Yes. Thanks.
     Which floor is my room on?

B   Your room is on the thirty-fourth floor in the Main Building,
     Mr. Ford.

B   How many stories does this hotel have?

B   Our hotel is thirty-eight stories high, and guest rooms are
     located between the seventh and the thirty-fourth floor.

G   My room is on the top floor, isn't it?
     It must have a beautiful view.
     It's so exciting.

B   You can see Mt. Bugak very clearly today.

Key Words

• Floor : 층
• View : 전망

Conversation 2 고객님의 방으로 안내해 드리겠습니다.

B   Ford 고객님, 고객님의 방을 안내해 드리겠습니다.
       엘리베이터는 오른쪽입니다. 이쪽으로 오십시오.

G   감사합니다.
       제 방은 몇 층입니까?

B   고객님의 방은 본관 34층에 있습니다.

G   호텔은 총 몇 층입니까?

B   저희 호텔은 총 38층이며, 고객님의 방은 7층과 34층 사이에 있습니다.

G   저의 방이 최고층에 있습니까?
       전망이 좋겠네요, 기대됩니다.

B   오늘은 북악산의 전망이 잘 보이실 겁니다.

 Point Expressions

• Show you to your room : 고객님의 방을 안내해 드리다.

• It's so exciting : 기대됩니다.

• You can see ~ : ~ 보이실 겁니다.

Conversation 3   **Explain the location of the emergency exit.**

B   Here we are.

This is your room, two-one-o-one, Mr. Ford.

Please allow me to explain the location of the emergency exit.

It is over there, where the green emergency light is lit.

G   By the way, is there an ice machine somewhere?

B   Yes, sir. Turn right at the corner over there, then go down the hallway, you will find the machine on your left.

 Key Words

• Emergency exit : 비상구

• Ice machine : 제빙기

• Hallway : 계단

Conversation 3 비상구의 위치를 설명해 드리겠습니다.

B 여기입니다. 2101호입니다, 고객님.
비상구의 위치를 설명해 드리겠습니다.
저쪽의 초록색 불이 보이는 곳이 비상구입니다.

G 그리고 제빙기는 어느 쪽에 있습니까?

B 예, 고객님.
오른쪽 끝에 있는 계단을 내려가시면 왼쪽에 있습니다.

 Point Expressions

• Here we are : 여기입니다.

• Allow : 허락하다, 용납하다.

• Green emergency light is lit : 초록색 불이 보이는

5형식으로 말하기

〈걷기〉 주제와 관련하여 '걷기의 장점은 무엇인가요?' 라는 문제에 답할 때, '걷기는 제가 건강을 유지하도록 도와줍니다.' 라고 답할 수 있어요. 이를 영어로 표현하면 다음과 같아요.

Walking helps me stay fit.

'주어가 ~을(~이) -하도록(-하는 것을) -하다'를 표현할 때는 위의 예문처럼 **[주어 + 동사 + 목적어 + 목적격 보어]**의 5형식 문장으로 말해요. 5형식 문장에서 자주 사용되는 동사에는 make(~을 -하게 만들다), help(~이 -하도록 돕다), see(~이 -하는 것을 보다/알다) 등이 있어요.

<u>Walking</u> <u>helps</u> <u>me</u>   <u>stay fit.</u> [5형식 문장]
  주어   동사 목적어 목적격 보어

● 문장 말해보기 ●

1. 그 음악은 저를 행복하게 만들었습니다.
⇒ The concert made me feel happy.

2. 저는 유명한 영화를 보았습니다.
⇒ I saw famous movie.

 Quiz

Q. 괄호 안의 표현을 사용하여 다음의 우리말 문장을 영어로 말해보세요.

1. 저는 엄마가 청소하시는 것을 도와드렸습니다. (my mother, clean)

   ⇒

2. 병원에 가는 것은 저를 긴장하게 만듭니다.

   (going to the hospital, feel nervous)

   ⇒

3. 그것은 거실을 더 환하게 만들었습니다. (the living room, bright)

   ⇒

4. 그녀는 자신의 학생이 결승전에서 우승하도록 도왔습니다.

   (her team, win the championship)

   ⇒

 Practical Point

Q. 괄호 안에 알맞은 말을 넣어 말해보세요.

1.

G   My room is on the top floor, isn't it?

It must have a beautiful (   ).

It's so exciting.

B   You can see Mt. Bugak very clearly today.

2.

G   Yes. Thanks.

Which (   ) is my room on?

B   Your room is on the thirty-fourth floor in the Main
Building, Mr. Ford.

Reading Comprehension

1.

Q   What is Mr. Ford's room number?

A   _____

_____

Door man/Bell man Service II

도어맨/벨맨 서비스

Door man/Bell man Service II
도어맨/벨맨 서비스

D (Door man) : 도어맨 | B (Bell man) : 벨맨 | G (Guest) : 고객

Conversation 1 **Here is your key card...**

> B (Open the door)
> Here your are.
> Would you like your luggage over here?
>
> G Yes, thank you.
>
> B Here is your key card, Mr. Ford.
> Please make sure to take it with you when you go out.
>
> G I'd like to have another key for my wife arriving later.
>
> B Certainly, sir.
> I will make another and bring it to you right away.

Key Words

• Luggage : 수하물

Conversation 1　**여기 고객님의 카드키입니다.**

B　(문을 열며⋯)
　여기입니다. 짐은 이쪽에 둘까요?

G　예, 감사합니다.

B　여기 고객님의 카드키입니다.
　외출하실 때에는 키를 소지하시기 바랍니다.

G　나중에 도착하는 아내를 위해 키 하나를 더 받고 싶습니다.

B　알겠습니다. 고객님.
　카드를 만들어 가져다 드리도록 하겠습니다.

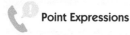 **Point Expressions**

● Bring it right away : 즉시 가져다 드리다.

Conversation 2 **I'm here to collect your luggage.**

B　Good afternoon, Mr. Ford. Thank you for waiting.
　　I'm here to collect your luggage.

G　Thanks.

B　You have two pieces of luggage. Is that correct, sir?

G　That's correct.

B　Are there any valuables or fragile items inside?

G　No.

B　We will keep your luggage at the Bell Desk on the first floor.
　　Please give this tag to anyone of our bell staff when you are
　　departing.

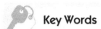

Key Words

• Valuables : 귀중품
• Fragile items : 깨지는 아이템들

Conversation 2 짐을 가지러 왔습니다.

B 안녕하세요, Ford 고객님. 기다려 주셔서 감사합니다.
   짐을 가지러 왔습니다.

G 감사합니다.

B 짐이 2개 맞습니까?

G 네, 맞습니다.

B 가방 안에 귀중품과 깨지기 쉬운 물건이 있습니까?

G 아니오, 없습니다.

B 1층 벨데스크에 보관해 드리도록 하겠습니다.
   출발하실 때 저희 직원에게 이 표를 주시면 짐을 드립니다.

 **Point Expressions**

• Collect your luggage 짐을 가지러 오다.

Conversation 3   **Are you checking out?**

D   Good morning, madam.
    Are you checking out?

G   Yes, I am going to Incheon airport by bus.

D   Do you have a reservation?

G   Yes, I do.

D   What time is your bus?

G   I'm taking the twelve thirty bus.

D   I will keep your luggage in the Cloakroom by the main
    entrance.
    Please be ready to board the bus 10 minutes before departure
    time.

G   Thanks.

D   You're welcome.

D   Have a nice flight back.
    We hope to see you again, madam.

Key Words

• Cloakroom : 호텔 벨데스크 짐 보관소

Conversation 3 체크아웃 하십니까?

D 안녕하세요. 고객님
   체크아웃 하십니까?

G 네, 버스로 인천 공항으로 갑니다.

D 예약은 하셨습니까?

G 네, 했습니다.

D 버스 시간이 몇 시입니까?

G 12시 30분입니다.

D 정문에 있는 물품 보관소에 짐을 맡겨 드리겠습니다.
   출발 10분 전에 버스정류장으로 오시면 됩니다.

G 감사합니다.

D 천만에요.

 Point Expressions

• What time is your bus? : 버스 시간이 몇 시입니까?

• We hope to see you again, madam. : 천만에요.

 **Grammar** 말하기 문법 　**어디에 무엇이 있는지 말하기**

〈장소〉 주제와 관련하여 '당신의 학교에 대해 묘사해 주세요?' 라는 문제에 답할 때, '저희 학교에는 도서관이 있어요.' 라고 답할 수 있어요. 이를 영어로 표현하면 다음과 같아요.

　　There is a library in my University.

'~이(가) 있다'를 표현할 때는 위의 예문처럼 [There + be동사 + 명사]의 형태로 말해요. 이 때 명사가 단수이면 There is를, 복수이면 There are를 써요. 특히 복수명사 앞에서 There is를 사용하지 않도록 주의합니다.

　　<u>There is</u>　<u>a library</u>　on the campus.
　　　　　　　　단수명사

　　<u>There are</u>　<u>three cafeterias</u>　on the campus.
　　　　　　　　　복수명사
　⇒ 복수명사 앞에서는 There are를 사용해야 해요.

• **문장 말해보기** •

　1. 저희 집 거실에는 에어컨이 있습니다.
　⇒ There is a Air conditioner in my living room.

　2. 학교에는 많은 벤치가 있습니다.
　⇒ There are many benches on the campus.

Quiz

Q. 괄호 안의 표현을 사용하여 **볼드체**로 된 우리말을 영어로 바꾸어 문장을 말해보세요.

1. 학교에는 **서점이 있습니다.** (a bookstore)

   ⇒ _____ on the campus.

2. 저희 동네에는 **많은 빌딩들이 있습니다.** (many buildings)

   ⇒ _____ in my neighborhood.

3. 제 방에는 **책들과 옷들이 많이 있습니다.** (many books and clothes)

   ⇒ _____ in my room.

4. 서울에는 **관광명소들이 많습니다.** (a lot of tourist attractions)

   ⇒ _____ in Seoul.

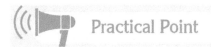

Practical Point

Q. 괄호 안에 알맞은 말을 넣어 말해보세요.

1.

D I will keep your luggage in the (   ) by the main entrance.

Please be ready to board the bus 10 minutes before departure time.

G Thanks.

2.

B You have two pieces of (   ). Is that correct, sir?

G That's correct.

Reading Comprehension

1.

Q   Has Mr.Ford's wife arrived the Bell desk?

A   _____

_____

Front Service I
프런트 서비스

Front Service I
프런트 서비스

R (Reception) : 프런트 직원 ┃ G (Guest) : 고객

Conversation 1 Welcome.

R Welcome to the Global Hotel. May I help you?

G Yes, my name is Schmidt, Arthur Schmidt.
And I booked a suite room for four nights.

R Yes, Mr. Schmidt, you booked a non-smoking double room
for four nights and you are planning to check out on
Wednesday?

G Yes.

R Could you fill out this form, please?

G Certainly.

 Key Words

• Suite room : 응접실(sitting room), 침실(bedroom), 욕실(bathroom), 주방(kitchen)
등의 시설이 갖추어진 고급 객실이다.

어서 오십시오.

R   안녕하세요. 글로벌호텔입니다. 무엇을 도와 드릴까요?

G   네, 저는 Schmidt, Arthur Schmidt입니다.
    그리고 스위트룸으로 4박 예약했습니다.

R   네, 고객님 금연층으로 스위트룸으로 4박 예약하셨고, 수요일 체크아웃 맞으십니까?

G   네, 맞습니다.

R   이 서류를 작성해 주시겠습니까?

G   알겠습니다.

Point Expressions

• Could you fill out this form, please? : 이 서류를 작성해 주시겠습니까?

Conversation 2 **May I have a print of your credit card...**

G (as finishing filling out the form) Here you are.

R Thank you very much, Mr. Schmidt.
May I have a print of your credit card, please?

G Yes, certainly. Here you go.
(presenting credit card)

R Thank you very much. (take a print)
Here is your card.

Key Words

• Print of your credit card : 신용카드 복사

Conversation 2 신용카드를 복사해도 되겠습니까?

G (서류 작성을 다 마치고)
여기 있습니다.

R 감사합니다, Schmidt 고객님.
고객님의 신용카드를 복사해도 괜찮으시겠습니까?

G 네, 여기 있습니다. (카드를 복사한다)

R 대단히 감사합니다. 여기 카드 있습니다.

 Point Expressions

• Here you are : 여기 있습니다.

• Here is your card : 여기 카드 있습니다.

Conversation 3   **Here is your key.**

R   Here is your key.

Your room is located on the twenty-eight floor of our New Wing.

G   Thank you.

R   You're welcome.

Our bellman will guide you to your room.

Have a pleasant stay, sir.

Key Words

• Bellman : 벨맨

Conversation 3   여기 고객님의 열쇠입니다.

R   여기 고객님의 열쇠입니다.
    고객님의 방은 신관 28층입니다.

G   감사합니다.

R   천만에요. 저희 직원(벨맨)이 안내해 드릴 겁니다.
    즐거운 시간 되십시오.

 Point Expressions

• Be located on : ~에 위치해 있다.

• Guide you to : 안내해 드리다.

• Have a pleasant stay, sir : 즐거운 시간 되십시오.

Conversation 4 **Anything from the refrigerator?**

G₁ I'd like to check out, please. Here is our key.

R Yes, sir. Anything from the refrigerator?

G₁ Yes, I had two cans of beer and that's it.
   (to G2) And you?

G₂ Well, I had a can of orange juice and a small bottle of brandy from the mini-bar.

G₁ Well, that seems to be it!

R Yes, sir, you had two cans of beer, a can of orange juice and a small bottle from the mini-bar, right?

G₁ That's correct!

Key Words

• Refrigerator : 냉장고
• Mini-bar : 미니바

Conversation 4   미니바 사용하신 내역이 있으십니까?

G₁ 체크아웃 부탁합니다. 키는 여기 있습니다.

R   네, 고객님. 미니바 사용하신 내역이 있으십니까?

G₁ 네, 맥주 2캔 먹었습니다.

    (다른 고객에게) 너는?

G₂ 나는 오렌지주스 그리고 미니바에서 작은 사이즈의 브랜디를 먹었습니다.

G₁ 그 외에는 이용한 것이 없는 것 같군요.

R   네, 고객님. 맥주 2캔, 오렌지주스, 그리고 미니바에서 작은 사이즈의 브랜디 맞으십니까?

G₁ 네, 맞습니다.

 Point Expressions

• That's correct : 네, 맞습니다.

it으로 긴 주어 짧게 말하기

〈요리하기〉 주제와 관련하여 '그 음식을 요리하기 좋아하는 이유가 무엇인가요?' 라는 문제에 답할 때, '재료를 구하는 것이 쉽습니다.' 라고 답할 수 있어요. 이를 영어로 표현하면 다음과 같아요.

It is easy to get the ingredients.

'재료를 구하는 것이'와 같이 주어의 길이가 길 때는 위의 예문처럼 주어를 맨 뒤로 보내고 대신 주어 자리에 it을 넣어 말해요. 길이가 긴 주어로는 위 예문의 to get ~처럼 [to+동사원형] 형태가 자주 사용됩니다.

It is easy to get the ingredients.
it   to+동사원형

• 문장 말해보기 •

1. 그들과 축구하는 것은 재미있습니다.
⇒ It is fun to play soccer with them.

2. 매일 운동하는 것은 중요합니다.
⇒ It is important to exercise everyday.

 Quiz

Q. 괄호 안의 표현을 사용하여 **볼드체**로 된 우리말을 영어로 바꾸어 문장을 말해보세요.

1. 저희 사무실은 조용해서, 휴식시간에 **휴식을 취하기가 쉽습니다.**
   (easy, rest)

   ⇒ My office is quiet, so _____

   during my coffee break.

2. 사원들을 위한 **오리엔테이션 세미나를 하는 것은 제 업무입니다.**
   (my job, conduct orientation seminars)

   ⇒ _____ for employees.

3. **부상을 막기 위해서는 알맞은 종류의 신발을 신는 것이** 중요합니다.
   (important, wear)

   ⇒ _____ the right type of footwear

   to prevent injuries.

4. 우리가 일을 할 때는 **함께 시간을 보내는 것이 어렵습니다.**
   (difficult, spend time together)

   ⇒ _____ when we are working.

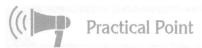 Practical Point

Q. 괄호 안에 알맞은 말을 넣어 말해보세요.

1.

G₁ Yes, I had two cans of beer and that's it.

( ) And you?

G₂ Well, I had a can of orange juice and a small bottle of

brandy from the ( )

2.

G Thank you.

R You're welcome.

Our bellman will ( ) you to your room.

Have a pleasant stay, sir.

3.

R ( ) you fill out this form, please?

G Certainly.

Reading Comprehension

1.

Q   Which floor is the guest going to stay?

A   _____

   _____

Chapter **8**

Front Service II
프런트 서비스

Front Service II
프런트 서비스

R (Reception) : 프런트 직원 | G (Guest) : 고객

Conversation 1 **Here is your bill could check it please?**

R Here is your bill if you could check it, please?

G Yes......, I made one hundred and thirty copies but it's not on the bill!
Could you check, please?

R Yes, sir. When did you make those copy?

G Half and hour ago.

R I see...... one moment, please.

R Thank you very much, sir. Here it is.
This is the bill, correct, sir?

G Yes.

Key Words

• Bill : 계산서(청구서)

Conversation 1 여기 고객님의 계산서입니다. 확인 부탁드립니다.

R 여기 고객님의 계산서가 있습니다. 확인 부탁드립니다.

G 네… 제가 130장을 복사했는데 이 비용이 계산서에는 포함되지 않았네요.
   확인 부탁합니다.

R 네, 고객님. 언제 복사를 하셨습니까?

G 30분 전에 한 것입니다.

R 알겠습니다. 잠시만 기다려 주십시오.

R 기다려 주셔서 감사합니다. 여기 있습니다. 계산서가 맞습니까, 고객님?

G 네.

 Point Expressions

• Here is your bill if you could check it, please? : 확인 부탁드립니다.

• Half an hour, ago : 30분 전에

Conversation 2   **May I have your signature, please?**

R   Here is your bill if you could check it, please?

G   Yes......, I didn't watch pay TV but I just pressed the button
   by mistake.

R   Yes, madam. I will erase that.
   Anything else?

G   No. This is fine. Here's my credit card.

R   Thank you very much. One moment, please.
   I'll reprint the bill.

R   Here you are. May I have your signature, please?

G   Certainly.

Key Words

• Pay TV : 유료 TV

Conversation 2 서명 부탁드립니다.

R   여기 고객님의 계산서입니다. 확인 부탁드립니다.

G   네…, 유료 TV는 보지 않았습니다. 실수로 버튼을 잘못 눌렀거든요.

R   네, 고객님. 그 비용은 제외하도록 하겠습니다.
     그 외에 (확인이) 필요한 부분은 없으십니까?

G   없습니다. 좋습니다. 여기 신용카드입니다.

R   감사합니다. 잠시만 기다려 주십시오, 계산서를 다시 뽑아 드리겠습니다.

R   여기 있습니다. 서명 부탁드립니다.

G   그러죠.

 Point Expressions

• May I have your signature : 서명 부탁드립니다.

Conversation 3   **Would you like to pay by cash or by credit card?**

G   I'd like to settle my account to date.

R   Certainly, madam.
     Mrs. Wong, room number two-zero-one-one?

G   Yes, How much is the bill?

R   It is four hundred ninety six thousand one hundred won.
     Would you like to pay by cash or by credit card?

G   With cash. Here you are.

R   Thank you very much.
     From five hundred thousand won?

G   Yes.

R   Here is your change, three thousand nine hundred won.
     And here is your receipt. Thank you very much.

Key Words

• Change : 거스름돈

Conversation 3 현금과 카드 중 어느 것으로 결제하시겠습니까?

G 계산서를 확인하고 싶습니다.

R 알겠습니다, Wong 고객님. 방 번호가 2011이십니까?

G 네, 얼마죠?

R 496,100원입니다.
  현금과 카드 중 어느 것으로 결제하시겠습니까?

G 현금으로 하겠습니다.

R 감사합니다. 500,000원 받았습니다.

G 네.

R 여기 거스름돈 있습니다. 3,900원입니다.
  그리고 계산서입니다. 대단히 감사합니다.

 **Point Expressions**

• Settle my account the date : 계산서를 확인하다.

Conversation 4   **I'm afraid that this card can't be accepted...**

G   Here's my credit card.

R   Yes, sir. A moment, please.

G   Sure.

R   Sir, do you have another card?

G   Yes, but why?

R   I'm afraid that this card can't be accepted.

G   What's wrong with it?

R   I can't tell, but this card is not being authorized.
     May be exceeding the limit ..... but if not, this happens quite
     often with foreign issued credit cards ...

G   All right. Here's another one. Try this.

R   Yes, sir. One moment, please.
     Yes! This time it is fine!

Key Words

• Foreign issued credit card : 해외 신용카드

Conversation 4 이 신용카드는 승인이 되지 않습니다.

G   여기 신용카드입니다.

R   네, 고객님. 잠시만 기다려 주십시오.

G   그러죠.

R   고객님, 다른 카드는 없으십니까?

G   예. 왜 그러죠?

R   대단히 죄송합니다만, 이 카드는 승인이 되지 않습니다.

G   무슨 문제라도 있습니까?

R   자세히 알 수는 없지만 카드가 승인이 안 됩니다.
    혹시 한도를 넘으신 건 아니신지…
    그렇지만 해외 신용카드에서 흔히 일어나는 일입니다.

G   알겠습니다. 여기 다른 카드입니다.

R   네, 고객님. 잠시만 기다려 주십시오.
    네, 다 됐습니다.

 **Point Expressions**

• This card can't be accepted : 이 카드는 승인이 되지 않습니다.

Conversation 5 **We hope to see you again in the near future.**

G1   Thank you, it was such a wonderful stay!

G2   Yes, we really enjoyed our stay.
     We're so sure that we'll be back again for our next visit!

R   Thank you very much, that is so nice of you.

G1   Oh, by the way, we're going to Ulsan by train and haven't
     purchased the ticket yet.
     Do you think that the tickets are available?

R   Yes, if there are some seats left.
     I think our concierge can help you with that.

G1   Very well, thank you.

R   Thank you very much, Mr. and Mrs. Osbourne.
     We hope to see you again in the near future.

G1   I'm sure you will. Good-bye.

R   Good-bye. Have a nice trip!

Key Words

• Next visit : 다음 방문

Conversation 5 빠른 시일 내에 또 만나 뵙게 되길 바랍니다.

G₁ 감사합니다. 멋진 시간이었습니다.

G₂ 네, 정말 즐거운 시간이었습니다.
우리는 다음 기회에 한 번 더 방문할 겁니다.

R 감사합니다. 그리고 즐거운 시간을 보내셨다니 기쁩니다.

G₁ 오, 그런데 우리는 울산행 고속 열차를 타야 하는데 표를 사지 않았습니다.
티켓이 있을까요?

R 네, 만약에 자리가 남아 있다면요.
저희 컨시어지에서 그 건을 도와드릴 수 있을 겁니다.

G₁ 좋습니다. 감사합니다.

R 대단히 감사합니다, Osbourne 고객님.
빠른 시일 내에 또 만나 뵙게 되길 바랍니다.

G₁ 물론입니다. 안녕히 계세요.

R 안녕히 가세요. 즐거운 여행되시길 바랍니다.

 Point Expressions

- If there are some seats left : 자리가 남아 있다면요
- We hope to see you again in the near future. : 또 만나 뵙게 되길 바랍니다.

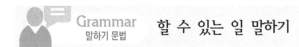

할 수 있는 일 말하기

〈집에서 보내는 휴가〉 주제와 관련하여 '휴가 기간에 집에 있는 것을 좋아하는 이유가 무엇인가요?' 라는 문제에 답할 때, '저는 집에서 쉴 수 있습니다.'라고 답할 수 있어요. 이를 영어로 표현하면 다음과 같아요.

I can relax at home.

'~할 수 있다'와 같이 어떤 일을 할 수 있는 능력이나 어떤 일이 일어날 가능성을 표현할 때는 위의 예문처럼 'can+동사원형'을 사용해 말해요. 과거에 대해 말할 때에는 can 대신 could를 사용합니다.

I can relax at home.
　can + 동사원형

I could relax at home last weekend. 저는 지난 주말에 집에서 쉴 수 있었습니다.
　could + 동사원형

• 문장 말해보기 •

1. 저는 제 방에서 쉽게 집중할 수 있습니다.

⇒ I can concentrate easily in my room.

2. 한 주는, 저는 집안일을 할 수 없었습니다.

⇒ One week, I couldn't do my chores.

Quiz

Q. 괄호 안의 표현을 사용하여 **볼드체**로 된 우리말을 영어로 바꾸어 문장을 말해보세요.

1. 그는 다양한 캐릭터를 **연기할 수 있습니다.** (play)

   ⇒ He _____ many different characters.

2. 제 집은 매우 넓어서 집 안에 많은 것을 **들여놓을 수 있습니다.**
   (keep)

   ⇒ My home is very large, so I _____ many things
   in it.

3. 저는 제가 만날 사람들과 **연락할 수 있도록** 휴대전화를 챙깁니다.
   (contact)

   ⇒ I pack a smart phone so that I _____ the people
   I will meet.

4. 저는 호텔 직원에게 제 항공편 일정을 **변경해줄 수 있는지** 물어보았
   습니다. (change)

   ⇒ I asked hotel concierge if they _____ my flight.

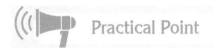

Practical Point

Q. 괄호 안에 알맞은 말을 넣어 말해보세요.

1.

G₁ Thank you, it was such a wonderful stay!

G₂ Yes, we really enjoyed our stay.

We're so sure that we'll be back again for our next

(   )!

2.

R Here you are. (   ) I have your signature, please?

G Certainly.

Reading Comprehension

1.

Q   When did the Guest make thirty copies?

A   _____

_____

2.

Q   Does Mrs. Wong paid by cash?

A   _____

_____

3.

Q   Where does the clerk work?

A   _____

_____

Housekeeping Service
하우스키핑 서비스

Housekeeping Service
하우스키핑 서비스

H (Housekeeping) : 하우스키핑 직원 | G (Guest) : 고객

Conversation 1 **I'm here to pick up your laundry.**

H Good morning, Mr. Oliveila. This is Housekeeping.
   I'm here to pick up your laundry.

G Ah, you came so quickly. It's not really yet.

H No problem, sir. I will wait.

G It's ready now. Here is everything.

H (look inside of the laundry bag and check the sheet)
   Certainly, sir.
   We will have these back by five o'clock this afternoon.

G I'm going out right now. I'd like you to deliver them to my
   room.

H Certainly, sir.
   Shall we hang them up inside the closet?

G Yes, that's a good idea. Thanks.

Key Words

• Laundry : 세탁물

Conversation 1 라운드리 가지러 왔습니다.

H 안녕하세요, Oilveila 고객님. 하우스키핑입니다.
   고객님의 라운드리를 가지러 왔습니다.

G 너무 빨리 왔네요. 아직 준비가 되지 않았어요.

H 기다리겠습니다.

G 준비됐습니다. 여기 있습니다.

H (라운드리백에 라운드리시트가 있는지 확인하고)
   네, 고객님 오늘 오후 5시에 배달해 드리겠습니다.

G 전 지금 나갈 건데요. 나중에 제 방으로 배달해 주세요.

H 그러겠습니다, 고객님. 고객님 옷장 안에 걸어두면 어떨까요?

G 네, 좋은 생각이네요. 감사합니다.

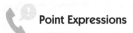

Point Expressions

• Deliver to room : 객실로 배달해 드리다.

Conversation 2 **I'm here to deliver your laundry.**

H This is Housekeeping.

Mr. Lee, I'm here to deliver your laundry.

G Thank you.

H Here you are, sir.

You requested we remove this stain, Unfortunately we couldn't.

Our supervisor tried to remove it by using a special method.

We are very sorry.

G Oh, no! Is there another way?

H We did our best...... If we try any further, the material itself may be damaged.

G I see...... It seems like all I can do is just give up.

H Thank you very much for your understanding.

Key Words

• Stain : 얼룩

Conversation 2 세탁물 배달 왔습니다.

H 여기는 하우스키핑입니다. 고객님의 세탁물을 배달하러 왔습니다.

G 감사합니다.

H 여기 있습니다. 고객님이 요청하신 세탁물의 얼룩은 저희 지배인이 노력해 보았으나 처리하지 못했습니다.
대단히 죄송합니다.

G 오! 안돼요.. 다른 방법은 없습니까?

H 저희는 최선을 다했습니다. 여기서 더 시도를 한다면 옷감이 손상될 수도 있습니다만.

G 알겠습니다. 그렇다면 어쩔 수 없죠..

H 이해해 주셔서 대단히 감사합니다.

Point Expressions

- We did our best :저희는 최선을 다했습니다.
- Thank you very much for your understanding. : 이해해 주셔서 대단히 감사합니다.

Conversation 3 **We are sorry for the inconvenience.**

H   Good afternoon, Mr. Brown.

Thank you very much for staying with us again.

We heard that the air conditioner isn't working properly.

G   I just arrived, came in, and tried to cool the room down.

But, it doesn't work with the panel at all.

H   I will check it right away.

H   There is something wrong with the panel.

Since it will take some time, we will prepare another room

for you.

G   Yes, I'll be working at the Business Center,

please let me know when the room is ready.

H   Certainly, sir. We are sorry for the inconvenience.

G   Please do it as soon as possible.

Key Words

• Air Conditioner : 에어컨
• Business Center : 비즈니스센터

Conversation 3   불편을 드려 대단히 죄송합니다.

H   안녕하세요, Brown 고객님. 다시 찾아주셔서 감사합니다.
하지만 고객님 방의 에어컨이 제대로 작동되지 않는다고 들었습니다.

G   도착해서 에어컨을 켰는데 작동이 되질 않습니다.

H   에어컨에 문제가 있습니다. 시간이 좀 걸릴 것 같습니다.
다른 방을 고객님께 준비해 드리겠습니다.

G   저는 비즈니스센터에 있으니, 방이 준비가 되면 저에게 알려주십시오.

H   알겠습니다. 불편을 드려 대단히 죄송합니다.

G   가능하다면 빠른 시간 내에 부탁합니다.

 Point Expressions

• It's not working : 작동이 되지 않는다.

We are sorry for the inconvenience. : 불편을 드려 대단히 죄송합니다.

Conversation 4 **If you need something else, please let me know.**

H   Good morning, Mr, Brown.

     I'm here for the turndown service.

G   Sorry? What's that?

H   I will prepare your bed for the night and refill the toiletries.

G   That's great. Please come in.

H   Thank you, sir.

     (after turning down the bed and refilling the toiletries)

     If you need something else, please let me know.

G   Well, the mineral water is running out.

     May I have a couple of bottles?

H   Mineral water, sir?

     Yes, I will bring them right away.

Key Words

- Turn Down Service : 방을 준비해 드리는 서비스
- Mineral Water : 생수

Conversation 4 더 필요하신 것은 없으십니까? 있으시면 알려 주십시오.

H 안녕하세요, Brown 고객님.
   턴다운 서비스입니다.

G 네? 그게 뭐하는 겁니까?

H 고객님이 주무시기 전에 방을 준비해 드리는 서비스입니다.

G 아, 좋습니다. 들어오세요.

H 감사합니다.
   (턴다운과 욕실용품을 리필해 드림)
   더 필요하신 것은 없으십니까? 있으시면 알려 주십시오.

G 물이 다 떨어져갑니다. 몇 병 더 주세요.

H 생수 말씀이세요? 가져다 드리겠습니다.

 **Point Expressions**

• Refill the toiletries : 욕실용품을 리필해 드리다.

Grammar
말하기 문법   시간 표현하기

〈조깅하기〉 주제와 관련하여 '당신은 언제 조깅을 하나요?' 라는 문제에 답할 때, '저는 주말마다 조깅을 합니다.' 라고 답할 수 있어요. 이를 영어로 표현하면 다음과 같아요.

I go jogging on weekends.

'~(때)에' 또는 '(언제)까지' 등의 시간을 표현할 때는 위의 예문처럼 전치사를 사용해서 말해요. 시간을 나타내는 전치사에는 at, on, in, during, for 등이 있고, 아래와 같이 사용됩니다.

- at (~에)   at 6 o'clock   6시 정각에
- on (~에)   on Saturday   토요일에
- in (~에)   in 1984   1984년에
- during (~동안)   during the holidays   휴가 동안

Tip! during과 for는 모두 '~ 동안'으로 해석되지만, during은 휴가나 방학과 같은 특정기간을 나타내는 표현 앞에, for는 며칠이나 몇 년과 같은 기간을 나타내는 숫자 앞에 옵니다.

• OPIc 문장 말해보기 •

1. 밤에, 저는 에어컨을 틀어야 합니다.

⇒ At night, I have to turn on the air conditioner.

2. 저희 회사는 1984년에 설립되었습니다.

⇒ My company was established in 1984.

Quiz

Q. 괄호 안의 표현을 사용하여 **볼드체**로 된 우리말을 영어로 바꾸어 문장을 말해보세요.

1. 저는 **미래에** 호텔에서 일하고 싶습니다. (the future)

   ⇒ I want to work for a hotel _____ .

2. 저는 글로벌 호텔에서 **3년 동안** 근무했습니다. (three years)

   ⇒ I have worked at Global Hotel _____ .

3. 저는 **일요일 오후마다** 볶음밥을 요리하는 것을 좋아합니다.
   (Sunday afternoon)

   ⇒ I like to make fried rice _____ .

4. 그는 **여행하는 동안** 사진을 많이 찍었습니다. (the trip)

   ⇒ He took a lot of pictures _____ .

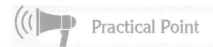

Practical Point

Q. 괄호 안에 알맞은 말을 넣어 말해보세요.

1.

H　Here you are, sir.

　　You requested we remove this (　　　　), Unfortunately we couldn't.

　　Our supervisor tried to remove it by using a special method.

　　We are very sorry.

G　Oh, no! Is there another way?

2.

H　Good morning, Mr. Oliveila. This is Housekeeping.

　　I'm here to pick up your (　　　　).

G　Ah, you came so quickly. It's not really yet.

Reading Comprehension

1.

Q   Where is Mr. Brown going to working?

A   _____

_____

2.

G   What does Mr. Brown order for the turndown service?

A   _____

_____

제 **2** 부

식음료 부문

Room Service

룸 서비스

Room Service
룸 서비스

R (Room Service) : 룸 서비스 직원 | G (Guest) : 고객

Conversation 1 **What time would you like to have your breakfast?**

R   This is room service, may I help you?

G   Yes, I'd like to order breakfast for tomorrow morning.

R   Certainly.
    May I have your name and your room number, please?

G   Sure, Plant, Bob Plant and my room number is seventeen eighteen.

R   Certainly, Mr. Plant. What time would you like to have your breakfast?

G   Yes, at seven, please.

R   Yes, breakfast at seven o'clock for Mr. Bob Plant, room number seventy eighteen?

G   No, room number one-seven-one-eight!

R   Oh, I'm sorry.

G   That's Okay.

Key Words

• Room Number : 객실번호

Conversation 1 조식은 몇 시에 원하십니까?

R 룸 서비스입니다. 무엇을 도와드릴까요?

G 내일 아침을 주문하고 싶습니다.

R 네, 고객님. 고객님 이름과 방번호를 알려 주십시오.

G 네. Plant, Bob Plant입니다. 제 방번호는 1718호입니다.

R 네, 고객님. 조식은 몇 시에 원하십니까?

G 7시에 부탁합니다.

R 네, 내일 오전 7시에 7018호 방 맞습니까?

G 아니요, 제 방은 1718호입니다.

R 오, 죄송합니다.

G 괜찮습니다.

 Point Expressions

• Order Breakfast : 조식을 주문하다.

Conversation 2   **May I repeat the order?**

R   Your order, please.

G   Yes, I'd like to have an American breakfast.
I'd like to have a glass of orange juice, scrambled eggs with bacon, two pieces of toast and decaffeinated coffee, if you have it.

R   Yes, sir. May I repeat the order?
A glass of orange juice, scrambled eggs with bacon, two pieces of toast and decaffeinated coffee, is that correct?

G   Yes, correct.

Key Words

• American Breakfast : 미국식 조식

Conversation 2   주문하신 내용을 확인해 드리겠습니다.

R   주문 받겠습니다, 고객님.

G   네, 저는 미국식 식사를 먹겠습니다. 오렌지주스 한 잔, 스크램블 에그, 베이컨,
토스트 두 조각, 디카페인 커피가 있다면 그걸로 주세요.

R   네. 주문하신 내용을 확인해 드리겠습니다.
오렌지주스 한 잔, 스크램블 에그, 베이컨, 토스트 두 조각, 디카페인 커피 맞습니
까?

G   네, 맞습니다.

 **Point Expressions**

• May I repeat the order : 주문하신 내용을 확인해 드리겠습니다.

Conversation 3 **Thank you for waiting, your breakfast is ready.**

R (Knock on the door)

G Who is it?

R This is room service.
Thank you for waiting, your breakfast is ready.

G (open the door) Come in.

R Thank you, madam.
Where would you like your breakfast?

G Here, by the bed, please.

R Certainly, a glass of apple juice, scrambled eggs with bacon, croissant and coffee, is this correct?

G Yes, perfect.

R Thank you very much.

Key Words

• Madam : 결혼한 여성의 존칭

Conversation 3 기다려 주셔서 감사합니다. 아침식사입니다.

R   (노크를 한다)

G   누구세요?

R   룸 서비스입니다. 기다려 주셔서 감사합니다.
    아침식사입니다.

G   (문을 열며) 들어오세요.

R   감사합니다, 고객님. 어디에 놓아 드릴까요?

G   침대 옆에 놔 주세요.

R   네, 고객님. 애플주스, 스크램블 에그, 베이컨 크라상, 그리고 커피 맞습니까?

G   네, 맞습니다.

R   감사합니다.

Point Expressions

• Breakfast is ready : 아침식사입니다.

Conversation 4 **May I have your signature on the bill?**

R   May I have your signature on the bill?

G   Sure. Here you are.

R   Thank you very much. And this is your copy.
Enjoy your breakfast.

G   Thank you. Oh, when it's finished, should I call room
service again, for picking up the dishes?

R   No, madam, just leave them outside the door, please.

G   Oh, that's easy. I'll do so.

R   Thank you very much. Have a nice day.

G   Thank you, I'm sure I will. The same to you.

R   Thank you very much, madam.

 **Key Words**

• Signature : 서명

Conversation 4 서명 부탁드립니다.

R 서명 부탁드립니다.

G 네, 여기 있습니다.

R 감사합니다. 계산서입니다. 즐거운 식사 되십시오.

G 감사합니다. 식사가 끝나면 룸 서비스로 전화해서 그릇을 치워 달라고 해야 합니까?

R 아니요. 고객님. 문밖에 두시면 됩니다.

G 오, 그래요. 그렇게 하죠.

R 대단히 감사합니다. 좋은 하루 되십시오.

G 감사합니다. 그러죠, 그쪽도 좋은 하루 되세요.

R 대단히 감사합니다.

 **Point Expressions**

• Leave them outside the door : 문밖에 두시면 됩니다.

장소 표현하기

〈자전거 타기〉 주제와 관련하여 '당신은 어디에서 자전거를 타나요?' 라는 문제에 답할 때, '저는 주로 공원에서 자전거를 탑니다.' 라고 답할 수 있어요. 이를 영어로 표현하면 다음과 같아요.

I usually ride my bike in the park.

'(장소)에' 또는 '~에서' 등의 장소를 표현할 때는 위의 예문처럼 전치사를 사용해서 말해요. 장소를 나타내는 전치사에는 at, on, in 등이 있고, 아래와 같이 사용됩니다.

- at (~지점에) at school 학교에
- on (~위에) on the subway 지하철에
- in (~안에) in the room 방 안에

• 문장 말해보기 •

1. 세종대학교는 군자동에 있습니다.
⇒ Sejong University is in Gunja.

2. 저는 회사에서 컴퓨터를 사용합니다.
⇒ I use a computer at work.

 Quiz

Q. 괄호 안의 표현을 사용하여 **볼드체**로 된 우리말을 영어로 바꾸어 문장을 말해보세요.

1. **학교에는** 많은 건물들이 있습니다. (the campus)

   ⇒ There are many buildings _____ .

2. **방 안에는** 침대, 책상, 그리고 의자가 있습니다. (the room)

   ⇒ I have a bed, a desk, and a chair _____ .

3. 저희는 주로 **집에서** 함께 저녁식사를 준비합니다. (home)

   ⇒ We usually prepare dinner together _____ .

4. 저는 주로 **지하철에서** 음악을 듣습니다. (the subway)

   ⇒ I usually listen to music _____ .

Practical Point

Q. 괄호 안에 알맞은 말을 넣어 말해보세요.

1.

R May I have your (   ) on the bill?

G Sure. Here you are.

2.

R Your order, please.

G Yes, I'd like to have an (   ).

I'd like to have a glass of orange juice, scrambled eggs with bacon, two pieces of toast and decaffeinated coffee, if you have it.

3.

R Yes, breakfast at seven o'clock for Mr. Bob Plant,

(   ) seventy eighteen?

G No, one-seven-one-eight!

Reading Comprehension

1.

Q What does the guest order as a breakfast?

A _____

_____

Chapter 11

Food & Beverage Service I
식음료 서비스

- **Conversation 1** : May I have your name, please?
- **Conversation 2** : I'm afraid the tables by the window are fully booked right now.
- **Conversation 3** : I will locate your guest, sir/madam.
- **Grammar**(말하기 문법) : 이유·시간·조건 말하기
- **Quiz**
- **Practical Point**
- **Reading Comprehension**

Food & Beverage Service I
식음료 서비스

W (Waiter/Waitress) : 웨이터/웨이트리스 | G (Guest) : 고객

Conversation 1 **May I have your name, please?**

W Good evening, sir/madam.

Do you have a reservation?

G Yes, I have a reservation for 7 o'clock.

W May I have your name, please?

(What name did you make the reservation under?)

G Kim Myunghak. I reserved a table for three.

W Oh, yes. I have your reservation here.

I'll show you to your table.

Could you please follow me?

G Thank you.

Key Words

• Table : 레스토랑의 예약된 자리

Conversation 1 어느 분 성함으로 예약하셨습니까?

W 안녕하십니까? 혹시 예약은 하셨습니까?

G 네, 7시에 예약했어요.

W 어느 분 성함으로 예약하셨습니까?

G 김명학으로 3명 예약했습니다.

W 아! 김명학 고객님, 7시로 3분 예약되어 있습니다.
제가 안내해 드리겠습니다.

G 감사합니다.

Point Expressions

• I'll show you to your table : 제가 안내해 드리겠습니다.

Conversation 2 **I'm afraid the tables by the window are fully booked right now.**

W   Here is your table.

Are you satisfied with table sir/madam?

G   Do you have any tables by the window?

W   I'm afraid the tables by the window are fully booked right now.

G   All right. Is this a smoking area?

W   I'm sorry, sir/madam. This is a non-smoking restaurant, but we do have designated smoking areas.

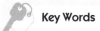

Key Words

• Smoking Area : 흡연구역

Conversation 2 창가 쪽 테이블은 이미 예약되어 있습니다.

W   이 테이블로 준비했습니다. 마음에 드십니까?

G   창가 쪽 자리는 없습니까?

W   죄송하지만 창가 쪽 테이블은 이미 예약되어 있습니다.

G   알겠어요. 이곳에서 담배 피울 수 있어요?

W   영업장 내에선 전 구역이 금연석입니다. 지정된 흡연 장소를 이용해 주시겠습니까?

 Point Expressions

● The table by the window are fully booked : 창가 쪽 테이블은 이미 예약되어 있습니다.

Conversation 3   **I will locate your guest, sir/madam.**

w   Hello. Welcome to the Global Hotel.

Are you looking for a guest, sir/madam?

G   Yes, I am. But unfortunately, I don't know what he/she looks like.

Could you help me find him/her?

w   Certainly, sir/madam. Could you please write down the person's name on the memo pad?

I will check for you.

G   Okay, that's great.

w   Could you please wait here?

I will locate your guest, sir/madam.

Key Words

• Person's name : 성명

Conversation 3　저희가 찾으시는 고객님을 안내해 드리겠습니다.

W　안녕하십니까? 찾으시는 고객님이 계십니까?

G　네, 그런데 얼굴을 모르는 손님을 찾는데 어떻게 하죠?

W　네, 고객님. 앞쪽에 준비되어 있는 메모란을 확인하시고 성명을 기재하시면 저희가 안내해 드리겠습니다.

G　기록했습니다. 그럼 부탁드릴게요.

W　네, 고객님 이 테이블에 앉아 계시면
　　저희가 찾으시는 고객님을 안내해 드리겠습니다.

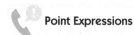 **Point Expressions**

• I'll locate your guest, sir : 저희가 찾으시는 고객님을 안내해 드리겠습니다.

이유 · 시간 · 조건 말하기

〈음악 감상하기〉 주제와 관련하여 '그 음악을 좋아하는 이유가 무엇인가요?' 라는 문제에 답할 때, '마음을 편안하게 해주기 때문에 그 노래가 가장 좋습니다.' 라고 답할 수 있어요. 이를 영어로 표현하면 다음과 같아요.

The song is my favorite because it is very relaxing.

'~이기 때문에'를 표현할 때는 위의 예문처럼 부사절 접속사 because를 사용해요. 부사절 접속사에는 이유를 나타내는 because(~이기 때문에) 외에, 시간을 나타내는 when(~할 때에), before(~전에), after(~후에), 그리고 상황을 가정하는 if(만약 ~라면)가 있어요.

If there is enough time, I visit the shopping district.

충분한 시간이 있다면 저는 상점가를 방문합니다.

• 문장 말해보기 •

1. 저녁식사 후에, 모두가 휴식을 취합니다.

⇒ After dinner, everyone relaxes.

2. 할 일이 아무것도 없다면, 저는 잠시 낮잠을 자는 것을 좋아합니다.

⇒ If there's nothing to do, I like to take a short nap.

 Quiz

Q. 괄호 안의 표현을 사용하여 **볼드체**로 된 우리말을 영어로 바꾸어 문장을 말해보세요.

1. **제가 신상품을 출시했기 때문에** 기억에 남습니다.

   (I, launch, a new product)

   ⇒ It was memorable _____ .

2. **만약 주변에 다른 사람들이 있으면** 저는 산만해집니다.

   (other people, around)

   ⇒ I get distracted _____ .

3. **저는 공포영화를 볼 때**, 비명을 크게 자주 지릅니다.

   (I, watch, a horror movie)

   ⇒ _____, I scream loudly.

4. **요리하기 전에**, 저는 주로 재료를 준비합니다. (I, cook)

   ⇒ _____, I usually prepare the ingredients.

((◖🔊 Practical Point

Q. 괄호 안에 알맞은 말을 넣어 말해보세요.

1.

G I don't have much time. I just want a (   ) meal.

Can you recommend anything simple on the menu?

W I would like to recommend pasta.

2.

G Yes, I am. But unfortunately, I don't know what he/she looks like.

Could you help me find him/her?

W Certainly, sir/madam. Could you please write down the

(   ) on the memo pad?

I will check for you.

3.

W May I have your name, please?

(   )

G Kim Myunghak. I reserved a (   ) for three.

Reading Comprehension

1.

Q   What does waiter advise to the guest?

A   _____

     _____

Food & Beverage Service II
식음료 서비스

- **Conversation 1** : Can you recommend anything simple on the menu?
- **Conversation 2** : I'll bring your order immediately.
- **Conversation 3** : Did you enjoy your meal?
- **Conversation 4** : Could you prepare a cake for us?
- **Grammar**(말하기 문법) : that과 if 이용해 말하기
- **Quiz**
- **Practical Point**
- **Reading Comprehension**

Chapter 12

Food & Beverage Service II
식음료 서비스

W (Waiter/Waitress) : 웨이터/웨이트리스 | G (Guest) : 고객

Conversation 1 **Can you recommend anything simple on the menu?**

G I don't have much time. I just want a quick meal.
Can you recommend anything simple on the menu?

W I would like to recommend pasta.

G How long would it take?

W It will take about 15minutes.
Is that all right, sir/madam?

G Yes, then I would like cream pasta with mushroom and
ham.

🔑 **Key Words**

• Quick meal : 간단한 식사

Conversation 1   간단한 식사가 무엇이 있습니까?

G   시간이 없어서 그러는데 간단한 식사가 무엇이 있습니까?

W   간단한 식사로는 파스타 종류가 있습니다, 고객님.

G   파스타는 만드는데 얼마나 걸립니까?

W   파스타를 만드는 데는 약 15분 정도 걸립니다.
     괜찮으십니까?

G   네, 그러면 햄 머쉬룸 크림파스타 1개 부탁합니다.

 **Point Expressions**

• Can you recommend ~ : 무엇이 있습니까?

Conversation 2 **I'll bring your order immediately.**

G Excuse me, this is not what I ordered.

W Oh, really? I'm truly sorry.
   What did you order, sir/madam?

G I ordered the American breakfast but as you can see, I have
   been served the continental breakfast.

W I'm sorry, sir/madam. I'll bring your order immediately.
   Could you wait just a moment?

G Okay.

Key Words

• Continental Breakfast : 유럽식 조식

Conversation 2 즉시 주문하신 것으로 바꿔 드리겠습니다.

G 이봐요, 내가 주문한 것이 아닙니다.

W 아! 그렇습니까?

   죄송합니다만, 어떤 음식을 주문하셨습니까?

G 아메리칸 아침식사를 주문했는데 보시다시피 컨티넨탈 아침식사가 나왔어요.

W 죄송합니다, 고객님. 즉시 주문하신 것으로 바꿔 드리겠습니다.
   잠시만 기다려 주시겠습니까?

G 알았어요.

Point Expressions

• I'll bring your order : 주문하신 것으로 바꿔 드리겠습니다.

Conversation 3 **Did you enjoy your meal?**

G Excuse, me. Could you bring me the bill?

W Certainly, sir/madam. Did you enjoy your meal?
Would you like to pay by cash or by credit card?

G I would like to charge it to my room.
Is it possible to charge here?

W Yes, sir/madam. Please sign here.

G Here? There you go. Thank you.

Key Words

• Cash : 현금 지불
• Credit Card : 신용카드 지불

Conversation 3   맛있게 드셨습니까?

G   이봐요! 계산서 좀 주세요.

W   네, 고객님. 맛있게 드셨습니까?
계산은 현금으로 하십니까? 아니면 카드로 하십니까?

G   룸 사인으로 하겠습니다. 테이블에서 계산이 됩니까?

W   물론입니다. 이곳에 서명 부탁드리겠습니다.

G   여기요? 감사합니다.

📞 Point Expressions

● Charge it to my room : 룸 사인으로 하겠습니다.

Conversation 4 **Could you prepare a cake for us?**

G   Today is one of my members' birthday.
Could you prepare a cake for us?

W   Of course, sir/madam. We can prepare a cake if there are
more than five people in your party.

G   Thank you.

W   How many candles would you like, sir/madam?

G   I need four big ones and five small ones.
Thank you.

Key Words

• Candles : 초

Conversation 4 **Could you prepare a cake for us?**

G 오늘 모임 중에 한 명이 생일인데 생일 케이크가 준비가 되나요?

W 물론입니다.
5분 이상 이용을 하시면 저희가 준비해 드립니다.

G 그럼 부탁드릴게요.

W 초는 몇 개를 준비해 드리면 될까요?

G 큰 것 4개, 작은 것 5개 준비해 주세요. 감사합니다.

Point Expressions

• Prepare a cake : 케이크를 준비하다.

that과 if 이용해 말하기

〈수영〉 주제와 관련하여 '수영의 장점은 무엇인가요?' 라는 문제에 답할 때, '수영의 장점은 모든 근육을 사용한다는 것입니다.' 라고 답할 수 있어요. 이를 영어로 표현하면 다음과 같아요.

The advantage of swimming is that it uses every muscle.

'~가 -하는 것'을 표현할 때는 위의 예문처럼 부사절 접속사 that을 사용해요. 명사절 접속사에는 that(~하는 것), if(~인지 아닌지) 등이 있어요.

The problem was that I forgot my password.

문제는 제가 비밀번호를 잊어버렸다는 것입니다.

• 문장 말해보기 •

1. 갑자기 저는 가족들이 보이지 않는다는 것을 알게 되었습니다.

⇒ Suddenly I realized that I couldn't see my family.

2. 제가 아직 등록할 수 있는지 아시나요?

⇒ Do you know if I can still enroll?

 Quiz

Q. 괄호 안의 표현을 사용하여 **볼드체**로 된 우리말을 영어로 바꾸어 문장을 말해보세요.

1. 문제는 **제가 면을 너무 오래 삶았다는 것**입니다.

   (I, overcook, the noodles)

   ⇒ The problem was _____ .

2. 저는 항공사 직원에게 **제 항공편 일정을 변경해줄 수 있는지** 물어보
   았습니다. (they, could change, my flight)

   ⇒ I asked the airline staff _____ .

3. TV 프로그램 구성에서 가장 큰 변화는 이제 **리얼리티 프로그램이 많
   이 있다는 것**입니다. (there, are, many reality shows)

   ⇒ The biggest change in TV program is _____
   _____ now.

4. 상사께서 **우리가 특별손님을 맞이하게 될 것**을 알려주셨습니다.

   (we, would have, a special guest)

   ⇒ My boss announced _____ .

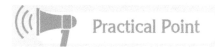

Practical Point

Q. 괄호 안에 알맞은 말을 넣어 말해보세요.

1.

w Certainly, sir/madam. Did you enjoy your meal?

Would you like to pay by cash or by credit card?

G I would like to (   ) it to my room.

Is it possible to charge here?

2.

G I ordered the American breakfast but as you can see,

I have been served the continental breakfast.

w I'm sorry, sir/madam. I'll bring your (   )
immediately.

Could you wait just a moment?

Reading Comprehension

1.

Q How long would it take a quick meal?

A _____

   _____

2.

Q What does the guest order?

A _____

   _____

Food & Beverage Service Ⅲ

식음료 서비스

- **Conversation 1** : Where can I buy some groceries?
- **Conversation 2** : I will check out for you, sir/madam.
- **Conversation 3** : Excuse me sir, but do you have another card?
- **Grammar**(말하기 문법) : 조동사로 질문하기
- **Quiz**
- **Practical Point**
- **Reading Comprehension**

Chapter 13 Food & Beverage Service Ⅲ
식음료 서비스

W (Waiter/Waitress) : 웨이터/웨이트리스 | **G** (Guest) : 고객

Conversation 1 **Where can I buy some groceries?**

G Where can I buy some groceries?

W The building right next to the hotel is the department store. You can buy some groceries over there.

G When are the hours of operation?

W It opens at 10:30 in the morning and closes at 8 o'clock in the evening.

G Thank you.

Key Words

• Groceries : 식료품

Conversation 1 식료품은 어디서 살 수 있습니까?

G 식료품을 사고 싶은데 어디서 살 수 있습니까?

W 바로 옆 건물이 백화점입니다.
   지하 1층에서 식료품을 구입하실 수 있습니다.

G 백화점은 영업시간이 어떻게 되나요?

W 네, 오후 8시까지 영업을 합니다.

G 알려줘서 고마워요.

Point Expressions

• When are the hours of operation? : 영업시간이 어떻게 되나요?

Conversation 2 I will check out for you, sir/madam.

G I had a breakfast in the buffet restaurant 'LS' this morning, but I seem to have forgotten my glasses on the table.

W What kind of glasses were they, sir/madam?

G They were black sunglasses with yellow frames.

W I will check it for you, sir/madam.
   We have it right here.

G That's great. Thank you.

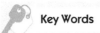

Key Words

• Sunglasses : 선글라스

Conversation 2 제가 한번 확인해 보겠습니다.

G 오늘 아침에 엘에스에서 식사를 하다가 안경을 테이블에 두고 온 것 같아요.

W 어떤 종류의 안경을 잃어 버리셨습니까?

G 노란색 안경테에 검은색 선글라스입니다.

W 제가 한번 확인해 보겠습니다.
   네, 여기 보관되어 있습니다.

G 다행이네요. 고마워요.

Point Expressions

• We have it right here : 여기 보관되어 있습니다.

Excuse me sir, but do you have another card?

G   Could I see the bill? I think you've overcharged me.
We only had 3 portions, not 4 portions.

W   Oh, I'm very sorry for the mistake, sir/madam.

G   No problem. So what is the total amount?

W   The total comes to 185,000 won.
How would yu like to pay?

G   By credit card. Here you are.

W   One moment, please.

W   Excuse me, sir, but do you have another card?
It seems your card has exceeded the limit.

G   Ohm really? Well, please try with this card.

W   We apologize for any inconvenience, sir/madam.

Key Words

• Portion : 몇 인분

Conversation 3 혹시 다른 카드가 있으십니까?

G 계산서를 확인할 수 있습니까?
   요금을 더 많이 청구한 것 같습니다.
   저희는 4인분이 아니라 3인분만 시켰는데요.

W 죄송합니다, 고객님.

G 괜찮습니다. 그래서 총 얼마죠?

W 총 185,000원입니다. 어떻게 지불하시겠습니까?

G 신용카드로 하겠습니다. 여기 있습니다.

W 잠시만 기다려 주시겠습니까?

W 혹시 다른 카드가 있으신가요, 고객님?
   카드 한도가 넘은 것 같습니다.

G 정말요? 그럼 이 카드로 한번 해 보시겠어요?

W 불편을 끼쳐 드려서 죄송합니다.

Point Expressions

• Do you have another card? : 다른 카드 있으신가요?

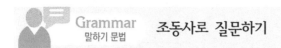

Grammar
말하기 문법　　조동사로 질문하기

〈롤플레이〉 문제에서 면접관이 '영화를 예약하기 위해 영화관에 전화해 질문하세요.' 라고 할 경우, '내일 아침 표를 예약할 수 있나요?' 라고 질문할 수 있어요. 이를 영어로 표현하면 다음과 같아요.

Can I reserve a ticket for tomorrow morning?

의문사 없이 '~할 수 있나요?'와 같이 질문할 때는 위의 예문처럼 [조동사 + 주어 + 동사] 형태의 조동사 의문문으로 말해요. 말하기 문법에서 자주 사용되는 조동사 의문문에는 Can/Could I ~?(제가 ~할 수 있나요?), Can/Could you ~?(당신은 ~해주실 수 있나요?), Do you ~?(당신은 ~하나요?) 등이 있어요.

Can/Could you help me register for the class?
당신은 제가 그 수업을 등록하도록 도와주실 수 있나요

•문장 말해보기•

1. 제가 당신과 약속을 잡을 수 있나요?
⇒ Can I make an appointment with you?

2. 그가 내일 시간이 있는지 아시나요?
⇒ Do you know if he has time tomorrow?

Quiz

Q. 괄호 안의 표현을 사용하여 **볼드체**로 된 우리말을 영어로 바꾸어 문장을 말해보세요.

1. 제가 치즈를 찾는 것을 **도와주실 수 있나요?** (you, help)

⇒ _____ me find cheese.

2. **당신은** 다른 종류의 소스를 가지고 **있나요?** (you, have)

⇒ _____ other types of cheese?

3. **제가** 20명의 테이블을 **예약할 수 있나요?** (I, reserve)

⇒ _____ a table for 10 people?

4. **당신은** 제가 아직 등록할 수 있는지 **아시나요?** (you, know)

⇒ _____ if I can still enroll?

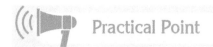

Practical Point

Q. 괄호 안에 알맞은 말을 넣어 말해보세요.

1.

G Could I see the bill? I think you've overcharged me.

   We only had 3 (   )

W Oh, I'm very sorry for the mistake, sir/madam.

2.

G Where can I buy some (   ) ?

W The building right nest to the hotel is the department store.

   You can buy some groceries over there.

Reading Comprehension

1.

Q   What is the guest's lost and found at the restaurant?

A   _____

    _____

제 **3** 부

Review

Activity I

Making dialogue

- **Topic 1** : Reservation Service(객실예약의 서비스)
- **Topic 2** : Operator's Service(교환원 서비스)
- **Topic 3** : Concierge Service(컨시어지 서비스)
- **Topic 4** : Door man/Bell man Service(도어맨/벨맨 서비스)

Activity I
– Making dialogue

Topic 1 **Reservation Service** (객실예약의 서비스)

● **Work with your partner!**

Situation :

In the Reservation Room of the 'Global Hotel'.

Reservation's, Miss. Lee is on duty:

She's change guest's reservation.

Topic 2   ## Operator's Service (교환원의 서비스)

● **Work with your partner!**

> Situation :
>
> In the Reservation Room of the 'Global Hotel'
> Operators, Miss Lee is on duty:
> She's connect guest's call to Reservation.

Topic 3   ## Concierge Service (컨시어지 서비스)

● **Work with your partner!**

> Situation :
>
> Concierge recommend tour attraction, Gyeongbok palace and Deoksu palace
> for a one day sightseeing trip to hotel guest

Topic 4   Door man/Bell man Service (도어맨/벨맨 서비스)

● **Work with your partner!**

Situation :

A bellman approaches the reception counter for the room key and to help a guest with his baggage.

Chapter 15

Activity Ⅱ

Making dialogue

- **Topic 1** : Front Service(프런트 서비스)
- **Topic 2** : Housekeeping Service(하우스키핑 서비스)
- **Topic 3** : Room Service(룸 서비스)
- **Topic 4** : Food and Beverages Service(식음료 서비스)

Activity Ⅱ
Making dialogue

Topic 1   **Front Service** (프런트 서비스)

• **Work with your partner!**

Situation :

To register a guest who has a reservation

Topic 2   Housekeeping Service

• **Work with your partner!**

Situation :

Joe, a Room maid, is Mr. Smith and his children.

They want to housekeeping staff pick up their laundry.

Topic 3   Room Service

• **Work with your partner!**

Situation :

A waiter is delivering breakfast to Room 1101.

He knocks first

Topic 4   **Food and Beverages Service**

● **Work with your partner!**

Situation :

In a restaurant.

The waiter bring guest order immediately

Appendix

부록

OPIc by Jenny Baek

1. OPIc 소개

1) OPIc 시험의 특징
- 개인 맞춤형 시험
- 응시자 친화형 실험
- 유창함에 중점을 둔 시험

2) ACTFUL에서 제시한 채점 기준
- 과제 및 기능 수행(Tasks and Function)
- 상황 및 내용(Context and Content)
- 정확성(Accuracy)
- 구성형태(Text Type)
- 발화용량(Production)
- 발화방법(Delivery)
- 유창함(Fluency)

3) OPIc 시험 공략법

① Background Survey 항목 선택 전략
- Background Survey에서 어떤 항목을 선택할지 미리 정해놓음
- 말하기 쉬운 항목 선택
- 답변이 유사한 항목 위주로 선택

② Self Assessment 난이도 선택 전략

- 자신의 말하기 수준과 비슷한 Self Assessment 난이도를 선택
- IL등급은 난이도 3, IM등급은 3~4, IH등급 이상은 난이도 5를 선택 권장

③ 답변 연습 전략

- 답변 패턴을 외워 여러 답변에 활용 연습
- 문법이 틀리더라도 말이 계속 이어지도록 연습
- 세부적인 사항을 구체적으로 처음–중간–끝/기승전결 형식으로 말하기 연습

2. Background Survey

1. 현재 귀하는 어느 분야에 종사하고 계십니까?

   ✓ 일 경험 없음

   1.1 현재 귀하는 직업이 있습니까?

   ✓ 아니오

   1.1.1 귀하의 근무 기간은 얼마나 되십니까?

   ✓ 첫 직장 - 2개월 미만

   ....

2. 현재 귀하는 학생이십니까?

   ✓ 아니오

   2.1 현재 귀하가 강의를 듣는 목적은 무엇입니까?

   ✓ 전문 지식을 향상시키기 위한 평생 학습

   2.2 예전에 들었던 강의의 목적은 무엇이었습니까?

   ✓ 전문 기술을 향상시키기 위한 평생 학습

   ....

3. 현재 귀하는 어디에 살고 계십니까?

   ✓ 독신자로서 개인 주택이나 아파트에 거주

   ....

4. 귀하는 여가 활동으로 주로 무엇을 하십니까? (두 개 이상 선택)

   ✓ 영화보기   ✓ 공연보기   ✓ 공원가기   ✓ 캠핑하기   ✓ 해변가기   ✓ 집안일 거들기

   ....

5. 귀하의 취미나 관심사는 무엇입니까? (한 개 이상 선택)

   ✓ 요리하기

   ....

6. 귀하는 주로 어떤 운동을 즐기십니까? (한 개 이상 선택)

   ✓ 자전거   ✓ 요가   ✓ 운동을 전혀 하지 않음

   ....

7. 당신은 어떤 휴가나 출장을 다녀온 경험이 있습니까? (한 개 이상 선택)

   ✓ 집에서 보내는 휴가   ✓ 국내여행

   ....

3. 고득점 취득 요령

1) 문단으로 구성하기

Q. What kinds of things do you usually do in order to maintain your health?
And tell me about the foods you eat to become healthy.
What are they?
Tell me in as much detail as possible.

✓ Introduction : There are many things that I do to be healthy these days.

✓ Body : ....

✓ Conclusion : So, I strongly recommend these things to my friend who wants to be healthy

Q2. Please tell me about a memorable day when you stay at home during your vacation. What happened? Who were you with? Tell me the whole story.

특별한 에피소드 말하기   ⇒ 기승전결의 구성

✓ 사건이 발생하기 전 상황

✓ 사건의 발생을 순서대로 전개

✓ 자신이 했던 활동을 구체적으로 말하기

✓ 사건 종료 후 본인의 생각과 느낌

2) 구체적으로 말하기

세부적인 사항을 구체적으로 부연 설명을 더해서 말하기

✓ I visited Jeju island.

✓ I visited Jeju island <u>which</u> is the biggest island <u>in</u> Korea <u>with</u> my family enjoy amazing beautiful beaches.

✓ I want to cancel our plan to go to the concert tonight because I have an emergent situation.

✓ I want to cancel our plan to go to the concert tonight because I have an emergency situation. <u>Yesterday</u>, I ate <u>a lot</u> <u>at</u> night <u>with</u> my sister, and I have a stomachache <u>seriously</u>. I can't move now.

4. OPIc Contents

≈ Common Construction of OPIc

01. 자기 소개하기 [Self Introduction]

Q. Let's start the interview now. Tell me a little about yourself.

 인사 – 이름 & 결혼 유무 & 사는 곳(나이 – 직업 – 회사) – 가족 사항 – 취미 – 마무리

Hello, Ava. Let me speak of myself a little./Um.. My name is JN, and I got married. So I live with my family in an apartment in Seoul which is the biggest city in Korea./There are four members in my family: my wife, my two sons and me. My wife is kind and my two sons are lovely. I love my family so much./In my free time, I like to watch TV at home all day long because I am a very laid back person. Plus, you know, watching TV makes me Relaxed a lot because I don't need to think anything while watching TV. Also, sometimes, I go to the park in my neighborhood with my family to go jogging or take a walk./That's all about me, and what about you, Ava?

Smart Words

• Good	• Diligent	• Optimistic	• Polite	• Flexible
	• Humorous	• Generous	• Confident	• Neat
	• Honest	• Easygoing		
• Bad	• Picky	• Aggressive	• Pessimistic	• Greedy
	• Sarcastic	• Cynical	• Stingy	• Arrogant
	• Stubborn	• Mean	• Bossy	

안녕, 에이바. 나에 대해서 알고 싶지? 내 이름은 JN이야. 난 현재 결혼을 해서 가족과 함께 한국에서 가장 큰 도시인 서울의 아파트에 살고 있어. 나의 가족은 아내, 두 아들 그리고 나까지 4명이야. 나의 아내는 아주 친절하고, 두 아들은 사랑스러워. 난 가족을 아주 많이 사랑해. 여가시간에는 난 느긋한

▶ 힌트는 270페이지에서 제공됨

편이라서 하루종일 TV 보는 것을 좋아해. 게다가 너도 알다시피 TV를 보는 동안은 그 어떤 생각도 할 필요가 없어서 휴식을 취할 수 있어. 그리고 가끔은 전 가족과 함께 동네에 있는 공원에 조깅이나 산책을 하러 가기도 해. 넌 어떠니?

Key Expressions

- I live with my family in an apartment in Seoul.
- There are four members in my family: my wife, my two sons and me.
- In my free time, I like to watch TV at home all day long.
- I am a very laid back person.
- Watching TV makes me relaxed a lot.
- That's all about me, and what about you, Ava?

02. 가장 좋아하는 장소 묘사하기

영화관/공연장/식당/쇼핑몰/공원/카페/술집/서점 등 응용 가능

Q1. You indicated in the survey that you like to go to the park. Describe your favorite park as much detail as possible. What make it so special?

 위치 – 크기 – 공원 안에 있는 것들 – 공원 주위에 있는 것들 – 공원에 대한 나의 생각

일반적인 정보–나의 상황

Well... about my favorite park? Okay. It is a very interesting question for me to answer because as you know, I like to go to the park in my neighborhood.

I always Try to go to the park but it is not that easy because I am busyworking. However, when I have my free time, I enjoy going there.

Describe your favorite park as much detail as possible.
What make it so special?

Let me speak of my favorite park as much detail as possible. It is called the Olympic Park and it's only 5-minutes-walk **(it's within 5 mins walking distance)** from my house. I usually go there with my friend Bona who lives at the same apartment complex./

The park is big and has a huge lake in the middle of the park./And there is a running track along the lake. There are many people **(who are)** walking, running, jogging, and riding a bike./Also, you can see many trees and beautiful flowers in the park. So this park is amazingly beautiful, especially In Spring because of many cherry blossom trees./

▶ 힌트는 270페이지에서 제공됨

공원을 좋아하는 이유

These are the reasons (For these reasons) I like to go there. So I strongly recommend the Olympic park. I am sure you will love it!

음... 내가 제일 좋아하는 공원? 알았어. 이 질문은 대답하기에 굉장히 흥미롭네. 왜냐하면 네가 말했듯이 난 우리 동네에 있는 공원에 가는 것을 좋아해.

난 항상 공원에 가려고 하지만 쉽지는 않아. 왜냐하면 난 일하느라 바쁘거든. 하지만 시간이 있으면 공원에 가는 걸 좋아해.

공원에 대해서 말할게. 그 공원은 올림픽공원이라고 불리는데, 우리 집에서 걸어서 5분밖에 안 걸려. 그리고 항상 같은 아파트에 사는 친구 Bona와 함께 공원에 가.

공원은 크고 중앙에는 큰 호수가 있어. 좋은 러닝 트랙이 호숫가를 따라서 이어져 있어서 많은 사람이 공원에서 산책하고 조깅하고 자전거를 타. 그리고 많은 나무와 예쁜 꽃들도 있어. 그래서 공원은 특히 벚꽃으로 가득한 봄에 굉장히 아름다워.

그래서 나는 그곳에 가는 것을 좋아해. 그래서 올림픽공원을 추천해. 내가 확신하는데, 너도 분명 올림픽공원이 좋을 거야.

Key Expressions

- As you know.
- When I have my free time.
- I enjoy going there.
- There are many people who are A, B, and C.
- You can see A and B in the park.
- I strongly recommend the olympic park.
- I am sure you will love it!

Q2. Describe one of the movie theaters that you often go to. Where is it? Why do you choose to go there over many others?

우리 집에서 5분 거리에 있는 백화점 5층(clean, pleasant, kind, well trained staff). 백화점 안에 위치한 영화관이라서 영화 관람 후 친구랑 쇼핑도 하고 옆에 있는 레스토랑에서 식사를 하기에 매우 편리함.

나의 상황

Oh, I have something to tell you about the theater. Actually, I sometimes go to movies, but it is difficult for me to do because I have a lot to do these days from my work. However, whenever I want to watch a movie, I usually go to theater in my neighborhood.

Describe one of the movie theaters that you often go to. Where is it?

The theater is on the 10th floor in the department store near my house. It takes only 5 minutes on foot. It's so close to my place. I usually get there with my friend Bona who lives at the same apartment complex.

Why do you choose to go there over many others?

There are some reasons that I go there. The theater is clean and pleasant. Also, the staff members are very well trained and quick to serve. They are very kind to the customers. Plus, as I told you before, the theater is in the department store, so I can do whatever I want such as doing some shopping, having a meal, and coffee without going outside. Can you imagine? How convenient! Ava~ I strongly recommend you to go there.

마무리-나의 생각

Anyways, for these reasons I love to go there rather than any others. If you have some time, visit my place you will love it.

오우, 나 영화관에 대해서 말할 게 있어. 사실 난 가끔 영화를 보고 싶지만 요즘 할 일이 많아서 어려워. 하지만 영화를 보고 싶을 땐 주로 우리 동네에 있는 영화관에 가.

영화관은 우리 집에서 근처에 있는 백화점 10층에 있어. 이곳까지는 걸어서 5분밖에 안 걸려서 꽤 가까워. 주로 같은 아파트에 사는 친구 Bona와 함께 영화관에 가곤 해.

그곳에 가는 이유가 몇 가지 있어. 그 영화관은 깨끗하고 쾌적해. 또한 스태프들이 잘 교육받았고, 응대도 빠르고, 친절해. 게다가 아까 내가 얘기했듯이 영화관이 백화점 안에 있어서 밖으로 나가지 않아도 쇼핑이나 식사, 커피 마시는 것 등 원하는 것은 무엇이든 할 수 있어. 상상이 돼? 얼마나 편리한지! 에이바, 난 네가 그곳에 가는 것을 추천해.

하여간 이러한 이유로 난 다른 곳보다 그곳에 가는 것을 좋아해. 만약 네가 시간이 있다면 그곳에 가면 좋을 거야.

Key Expressions

- The theater is on the 5th floor in the department store.
- It takes only 5 minutes on foot.
- There are some reasons that I go there.
- I strongly recommend you to go there.
- For these reasons I love to go there rather than any others.

03. 자전거 묘사하기

> **Q1.** Can you tell me about your bicycle? What does it look like? Where did you bike it? Please describe your bicycle in as much as possible.

🖉 나의 정보

All right~! My bike... OK... Let me see... My bicycle is ...well... just a city bike. So you can see this kind of bike everywhere. I bought it at a bike shop which is located on the second floor of Central Department Store which only takes 5minutes on foot.

🖉 Can you tell me about your bicycle? What does it look like? Where did you bike it?

It's blue and white... And it has two wheels. And there is a small black basket in front of the bike. Also, it has a big comfortable seat...
You know, it's not a new one. But it's very nice and clean. So I like it.

🖉 마무리

That's it. What about you, Ava? Do you have any bike? Then can you tell me about it?

알았어... 내 자전거... 좋아... 좀 생각해보자. 내 자전거는... 흠...그냥 도시형 자전거야. 그래서 이 종류를 어디서든 볼 수 있어. 나는 걸어서 5분 정도 걸리는 센추럴 백화점 2층에 있는 자전거 전문점에서 구입했어.

▶ 힌트는 270페이지에서 제공됨

이건 파란색과 흰색이 있고, 그리고 바퀴가 두 개야. 그리고 자전거 앞쪽에 작은 검은색 바구니가 있어. 또한 큰 편한 좌석이 있어. 알지? 이거 새건 아니고 그런데 좋고 깨끗해. 그래서 난 이게 좋아.

이게 다야. 에이바, 넌 어때? 너 자전거 갖고 있어? 그러면 나한테 얘기해줄래?

Key Expressions

- There is a small black basket in front of the bike.
- It has a big comfortable seat...
- What about you, Ava?

Q2. Let's talk about your bicycle routine. What kind of things do you do before and after riding a bicycle? Tell me about your typical bicycle routine from the beginning to the end.

나의 상황

I typically ride a bike at Central Park whenever I have my free time. But these days I have a lot to do from my work so I can't. I usually ride a bike with my friend JJ, who lives in the same apartment complex. While riding a bike alone, most of time I listen to Classic music on my smart phone, because it makes me happy.

Let's talk about your bicycle routine. What kind of things do you do before and after riding a bicycle?

Before riding a bike, I usually stretch my body. After my stretching, I ride a bike until I get rid of my stress.

Then...well... After riding a bike, I usually go to a sauna to relax.

That's it.

나는 일반적으로 시간이 날 때 센추럴 공원에서 자전거를 타는데 요즘은 일이 많아서 그러지 못해. 나는 주로 같은 아파트에 사는 친구 JJ랑 자전거를 타. 자전거를 혼자 탈 땐 대부분 내 핸드폰으로 클래식음악을 들어 왜냐하면 행복해지거든. 자전거 타기 전에 난 일반적으로 스트레칭을 해. 스트레칭 후에는 스트레스가 풀릴 때까지 자전거를 타.

그리고... 흠,.... 자전거를 타고 나선, 나는 긴장을 풀기 위해 사우나를 가지.

이게 다야.

▶ 힌트는 270페이지에서 제공됨

Key Expressions

- I typically ride a bike at Central Park whenever I have my free time.
- While riding a bike alone, most of time I listen to Classic music.
- I wear a casual training suit but when the weather gets colder, I put an extra jacket on me.
- I always make sure to wear comfortable running shoes.
- Before riding a bike I usually stretch my body.
- After my stretching, I ride a bike until I get rid of my stress.

Q3. When and how were you interested in riding a bicycle? Was there any special reason? How did you learn to ride it? Who taught you? Discuss your memorable experience in as much detail as you can.

나의 정보

Wow~ too many questions to answer. About 10 years ago, I used to have very serious back pain, because I was overweight.

When and how were you interested in riding a bicycle? Was there any special reason? How did you learn to ride it? Who taught you?

At that time, my friend JJ who lives at the same apartment complex suggested riding a bike with me. you know... She is a professional biker. That's right. She taught me how to ride a bike. Now! After 10 years, I feel much healthier. Can you believe it?

마무리

Also, riding a bike is good for my mental health because it helps me relieve my stress. Overall, when I have too much stress, or need some time to think, riding a bike is the best exercise.

▶ 힌트는 270페이지에서 제공됨

와우~ 답할 거 정말 많은데... 한 10년 전인가? 심각한 요통이 있었어. 왜냐하면 나 체중이 많이 늘었었거든.

그때, 같은 아파트에 사는 내 친구 JJ가 자전거를 같이 타자고 제안했었어. 내가 말했나? 얘는 전문적으로 자전거 타는 사람이야. 뭐 아무튼... 얘가 나한테 자전거 타는 법을 가르쳐 줬고, 지금, 10년이 지나서, 난 훨씬 건강해진 느낌이야. 믿을 수 있겠어?

또한 자전거 타는 것은 내 정신 건강에도 좋아. 왜냐하면 스트레스 해소가 되거든. 전반적으로 내가 스트레스를 많이 받거나 아니면 생각할 시간이 좀 필요할 땐, 자전거 타는 게 가장 좋은 운동 같아.

Key Expressions

- I used to have very serious back pain, because I was overweight.
- My friend suggested riding a bike with me.
- Riding a bike is good for my mental health because it helps me relieve
- My stress.

04. Role-play

Type 1. 질문하기 정보요청 - 초대 약속관련 핵심패턴

> Q1. Let me give a situation for you to act out. A friend wants to go
> jogging with you. Call your friend to go jogging. Ask him or her
> 3 or 4 questions about jogging.

인사

⇒ Hello, is this JK? This is JJ speaking.
How is it going? Cool. I'm good.

전화 건 목적

⇒ I believe you want to go jogging with me this weekend, right? That's
why I am calling you. Before we go for a jog. I want to ask you some
questions. Do you have some time? Good!

질문 1

⇒ First, where do you want to go jogging?
I like jogging at Central Park near house.
I like there because there are a lot of trees and beautiful flowers, a
variety of exercising equipment and a special running track alongthe
river. I strongly recommend this park.

질문 2

⇒ Also, when do you want to go jogging? Oh! Saturday? Not bad. What
time shall we meet then?
Let me think. I prefer to jog in the morning, what about you?

▶ 힌트는 270페이지에서 제공됨

질문 3

⇒ Oh! One more question.
If I have some problem to keep this appointment, what should I do?
Do you want me to call you right away?
oh! Cool! I got it.

> Q2. Let me give a situation for you to act out. You just moved into
> a new house and want to purchase new furniture. Call a furniture
> store and ask three or four questions about the furniture you want
> to buy.

인사/전화 건 목적

⇒ Hello, is this ABC furniture Store? This is JJ speaking. I have just
moved into a new house and I need a lot of furniture to buy.But I have
such a limited budget and it's kind of urgent.
I need to buy a bed in a hurry. That's why I'm calling you. Before I
decide to buy one, I would like to ask you some questions. Do you
have some time? Ok! Cool.

질문 1

⇒ What kinds of bed do you have? I am looking for something
modern, simple, and stylish.
How much is it? Thousand dollars~ It's kind of expensive. Ok.

질문 2

⇒ I also would like to buy a bed side table as well. Is there
anything you want to recommend? you do? How much is it then? 200$?
I guess that's will do.

▶ 힌트는 270페이지에서 제공됨

▨ 질문 3

⇒ Um... one more... If I pay in cash? Wow, OK! How much? 10%? Perfect! That's fantastic. What about delivery? How long does it take to be delivered? Is there any extra shipping cost to pay?
No~ That sounds good.

▨ 질문 4

⇒ Oh! Last question! Um... If I have some problem to use this product, what should I do? Do you want me to call you right away?
Do I need my receipt? If I want to cancel this product. is there any cancelation fee? ok.

▨ 마무리 문장

⇒ Thank you for taking your time. I really appreciate it. bye.

04. Role-play

Type 2. 상황대처하기

>Q1. Let me give a situation for you to act out. You are supposes to go to the park with your friend but you can't. Call your friend to explain the situation. Give 3 or 4 Suggestions.

🖊 인사

⇒ Hello, is this Jk? This is JJ speaking. How is it going? Cool. I'm good.

🖊 전화를 건 목적

⇒ I believe we were supposed to go to the park, right? But Um.. I have some situation. I am sorry to tell you this. But I never expected it would happen. Last night, I was getting ready to go to sleep. All of a sudden, I started to have a stomach ache. At first, I thought it was going to be ok, It was cried..... Oh! My Gosh! I didn't know what to do. I was totally lost. Anyways, I was taken to hospital and a doctor told us it was a food poison. I had no idea where it came from, though. Anyways, I'm still in hospital because I need some check up to do so I don't think I can go to the park with you.

🖊 제안 1

⇒ If you don't mind, could you call JD? Instead of me? She might have time for you. Actually, she likes going to park a lot. I am sure she will say yes or should I call and ask her? Or we can go to the park next time. What do you think?

▶ 힌트는 271페이지에서 제공됨

📞 제안 2

⇒ If you want to go to the park next week, that will be really good. By the way Um.. I want to buy dinner sometime next week,too. How does it sound? OK. That's good. Thank you so much your understanding. You are an angel!

📞 마무리

⇒ Then, I will call you back after I talk to JD. Bye~

> Q2. Upon arriving at the theater, you realized that you have ticket for the wrong movie. Explain your situation to the ticket seller and thenmake 2 or 3 suggestion that will help you resolve your problem.

📞 인사

⇒ Hello, Are you the person in charge of reservation?
Listen! I mean...

📞 사정 설명

⇒ I have some problems here. I hope you can understand this is urgent. Yesterday I booked 2 tickets the movie called Les Miserables. It starts at 7. I have hey look at this. These tickets are wrong. These are not for Les Miserables.

📞 속상한 마음 표현

⇒ I am very upset about this situation and hope you understand how urgent this matter is.

🖋 요구사항 1

⇒ Actually, I want to exchange them as soon as possible. It's my favorite movie and my friend wants to watch it for a long time.

🖋 요구사항 2

⇒ If it is not possible, then, Please let me exchange or get a refund right away.

🖋 마무리

⇒ Please take care of this as soon as possible, Thank you in advance.

05. 은행에서 계좌 오픈하는 방법 말하기 [방법 말하기 1]

Q. Now tell me about the process of opening a new bank account.
Describe the whole procedure starting with when you first step into
the bank.

일반 정보

Do you really hate me Ava? It's been a very long time. A bank...
bank account I need some time. OK, I think it's not complicated to
open a new bank account in Korea even to the foreigners.

Now tell me about the process of opening a new bank account. Describe the whole procedure starting with when you first step into the bank.

First, when you enter the bank, you have to get a number ticket from the
Q-machine and wait for your turn sitting on a sofa. When you see your
turn on the signboard, it's time to get served.

You need to show your photo ID such as your passport or driver's license,
fill out the form, and the teller does everything for you to open a bank
account. You just wait. Oh~, while waiting, you can set up your PIN# for
your bank and then, you can sign your name on the bankbook.

마무리-요약

That's it! It's the process to open a new bank account in Korea.
What about your country, Ava?

에이바! 당신 나를 싫어하는 게 분명 한 것 같아. 오래됐는데... 은행... 내 생각에 한국에서 은행 계좌를
개설(오픈)하는 것은 복잡하지 않아 심지어 외국인들도.

▶ 힌트는 271페이지에서 제공됨

먼저 은행에 들어가면 번호표를 뽑아. 그리고 소파에 앉아서 본인 순서를 기다려. 사인보드에 본인의 번호표가 뜨면, 직원에게 가서 준비해야 될 서류들이 몇 가지 있어.

먼저 여권이나 운전면허증과 같은 유효한 신분증을 직원에게 보여줘. 그리고 신청서를 작성해. 그럼 직원이 새로운 계좌 개설(오픈)을 위해서 모든 것을 해 줄 거야. 기다리는 동안, 은행 계좌의 비밀번호도 설정해. 그리고 통장에 사인을 해.

이게 다야! 그래서 한국에서 은행 계좌를 오픈하는 건 쉬워. 에이바, 너희 나라는 어때?

Key Expressions

- When you see your turn on the signboard, it's time to get served.

- What about your country, Ava?

06. 재활용하는 방법 말하기 [방법 말하기 2]

Q. Tell me about the recycling program in your country.
How do people recycle waste materials?

한국의 상황

Oh my God! Do you hate me Ava? It's a very hard question for me to answer. I really have nothing to say about your question, however, I will try. Everyone should recycle in Korea now. So in the public place such as subway stations, schools, or department stores, we can see two trash bins. one is for trash, and the other is for recycling but it's very hard for me to say.

Tell me about the recycling program in your country. How do people recycle waste materials?

So, let me tell you about how I recycle at home. In my case, I live in an apartment. Fortunately, there is a place to recycle on the first floor of the building. So first, I recycle cans, bottles, paper, or vinyl at home. I have a big yellow recycle bag in which I can put things separately. I gather things to recycle for a week. And I think it's every Sunday, I go to the recycle place as I told you before, and I put them into the boxes. All boxes have a name tag such as can, paper, or plastic, so I just put things into the right box.

마무리-본인 생각

Sometimes, I don't want to do it because it bothers me a lot. Anyways, this is my story. What about yours, Ava?

▶ 힌트는 271페이지에서 제공됨

음... 이 질문에 대해서는 말할 게 없지만 한 번 해볼게. 한국에서는 모두가 재활용을 해야만 해. 그래서 지하철역, 학교, 혹은 백화점 같은 공공장소에서 우린 2개의 쓰레기통을 볼 수가 있는데 하나는 일반쓰레기용이고 다른 하나는 재활용 쓰레기통이야.

그래서 내가 집에선 어떻게 재활용을 하는지 말해줄게. 내 경우엔 아파트에 살고 있어. 운이 좋게도, 아파트 1층에 재활용을 하는 장소가 있어. 그래서 먼저 캔, 병, 종이, 혹은 비닐들을 집에서 먼저 분리수거해. 재활용품들을 일주일 동안 여기에 모아. 주로 매주 일요일에 1층으로 가서 그곳에 있는 박스에 이것들을 넣어. 모든 박스에는 캔, 종이, 플라스틱이라는 이름표가 있어서, 맞는 박스에 넣기만 하면 돼. 가끔씩 이 일이 귀찮아서 하고 싶지 않을 때도 있어. 넌 어때 에이바?

Key Expressions

- In the public place such as subway stations, schools, or department stores, we can see
- Two trash bins.
- One is for trash, and the other is for recycling.

07. 이슈 이야기하기

Q1. Nowadays, people travel more than ever. Tell me about some issues people are interested in and care about most.

We are now living in a global society, and we have some issues to consider before traveling abroad.

To name some major issues, most importantly, you should consider safety. You must avoid the countries or cities that are threatened by terrorism. Also, you might have to eliminate the places from your lists where the natural disaster frequently occur. The bottom line is that safety should be the top priority when you travel. Another important thing you have to consider is that you need to be familiar with the cultures of the country you're going to travel. You have to know the taboos of the country and be careful not to violate them.

We learn a lot when traveling for sure. But I think we also learn many things while preparing for the travel.

▶ 힌트는 271페이지에서 제공됨

Q2. Tell me about the issues about housing in your country. What issues are told in broadcasting and news?

Housing is one of the most popular topic among Korean. And, nowadays, there are some issues regarding housing market.

First of all, growing concerning for an explosion of the rent is most noticeable in Korea. Unlike USA, we rent a house for an year with some deposit, and we call this housing system "전세." The price for this kind of rent has been increasing for the last couple of years. On the contrary, the housing price has been dropping. The housing market used to be booming about 10 years before, and many people bought houses with a huge mortgage. However, now those who had bought houses with mortgages express concerns about debts.

Koreans tend to consider it important to own a house. With these unique cultural environment, we often have housing issues.

08. 가장 좋아하는 장소 비교하기

> **Q1.** Please compare the movie theaters you often go to. How has the places changed over the years?

🖉 나의 과거 상황

Oh my god it's very hard question and it's very difficult for me to answer because when I was young there was no theater in my neighborhood. I didn't go to movie theater because I didn't have any money. I was very poor.

So I guess... Let me describe the movie theater which I often go to.

🖉 Please compare the movie theaters you often go to.
How has the places changed over the years?

The theater is on the 5th floor in the department store near my house. It takes only 5 minutes on foot. It's so close to my place! I usually get there with my friend JJ who lives at the same apartment complex.

There are some reasons that I go there. Um... The theater is clean and pleasant. Also, the staff members are very well trained and quick to serve.

They are very kind to the customers as well. As I told you before, the theater is in the department store, so I can do whatever I want such as doing some shopping, having a meal and coffee without going outside. Can you imagine?

How convenient! Ava~ I strongly recommend you to go there.

▶ 힌트는 271페이지에서 제공됨

마무리

If you go there, I am pretty sure you will love it as well.

어머나, 세상에. 이건 힘들고도 답하기 어려운 질문이야 왜냐면 내가 어렸을 때 우리 동네에는 영화관이 없었어. 어릴 때는 돈도 없어서 영화관을 가지 못했어. 나는 가난했었어. 자 추측해봐... 내사 자주 가는 극장을 묘사할게.

나 영화관에 대해서 말할 게 있어. 영화를 보고 싶을 땐 주로 우리 동네에 있는 영화관에 가. 영화관은 우리 집에서 근처에 있는 백화점 5층에 있어. 이곳 까지는 걸어서 5분밖에 안 걸려서 꽤 가까워. 주로 같은 아파트에 사는 친구 JJ와 함께 영화관에 가곤 해.

그 곳에 가는 이유가 몇 가지 있어. 그 영화관은 깨끗하고 쾌적해. 또한 스태프들이 잘 교육받았고, 응대도 빠르고, 친절해. 게다가 아까 내가 얘기했듯이 영화관이 백화점 안에 있어서 밖으로 나가지 않아도 쇼핑이나 식사, 커피 마시는 것 등 원하는 것은 무엇이든 할 수 있어. 상상이 돼? 얼마나 편리한지! 에이바, 난 네가 그곳에 가는 것을 추천해.

하여간 이러한 이유로 난 다른 곳보다 그 곳에 가는 것을 좋아해. 만약 네가 시간이 있다면 그곳에 가면 좋을 거야.

Key Expressions

- There are some reasons that I go there.

OPIc Vocaburary

🖋 주제: 직장

be responsible for

I am responsible for the confidential documents in our company.

work from home

These days, more and more people are working from home.

be out on business

he is out on business and will come back to the office at 3.

report on the progress

ABC has a lot of duties reporting on the progress.

🖋 주제: 일상생활

surrounding

ABC park was designed to harmonize with surroundings.

easy to handle

This mobile device has many easy functions to handle.

move in next door

The new family moved in next door last month.

take out the trash

My duty in my house is take out the trash and recycle materials on a weekly.

🖋 주제: 취미생활

on the way to work

I listen to my favorite music with my MP3 player on the way to work.

invite the neighbors over
Sometimes, my family invites the neighbors over to my house
to have dinner together.

every other day
My mother shops every other day in the local grocery shop.

be first interested in
I was first interested in chess in middle school.

make a big impact on
The autobiography of S J made a big impact on my life.

rarely have a chance to
Many applicants rarely have a chance to apply for the overseas
language program.

go to market
My wife and I get up early to go to market on weekends.

enjoy the scenery
My room is a excellent place to relax and enjoy the scenery
from the window.

be far away
The library I usually visit in my neighborhood is far away
from my house.

brilliant performance
Her brilliant performance produced an everlasting impression
and touched the audience.

get away from

Through the short trip, we could get away from daily routine at least for a while.

complimentary ticket

I watched a music concert for the first time with a complimentary ticket.

cinema complex

The cinema complex in my neighborhood has not only a movie theater but also a nice restaurant.

suit my tastes

Visiting the modern art exhibition suits my tastes.

주제: 여가활동

regardless of genre

Regardless of genre, all movies have certain elements in common.

purchase in advance

We can get a discount if we purchase the ticket at least 2weeks in advance.

dice → chop → mince

My wife minced vegetables and mixed them to make bibimbap for dinner.

rewarding

My musical experience in school has been very rewarding.
housewarming party

I am planning to have a housewarming party with coworkers.

sing along

My younger brother can sing along with all kinds of the
latest korean pop songs.

theatergoer

My friends usually call me a theatergoer whenever I go to the movies.

주제: 여행

travel itinerary

I finally completed the travel itinerary to italy.

accommodations

are the air fare and accommodations included in that price?

tourist attraction

The newly built building has become a tourist attraction.

sightsee

There are many places to sightsee near the hotel I stay in.

toiletries

Where is the nearest store where I can buy toiletries?

first-aid-medicine

Don't forget to get some first -aid medicine and buy
travel insurance.

souvenir

I spent the whole afternoon buying souvenirs for friends.

주제: 스포츠

aerobic exercise

To lose weight, you need to do some A E like swimming.

anaerobic exercise

score a point

J could not score a point against korea.

sporting equipment

You should be cautious when using sporting equipment.

workout outfit

I go jogging at the riverside wearing a workout outfit every Sunday.

end in a tie

The game end in a tie, 2 to 2.

a national team

주제: 인물묘사

good-tempered

She is good tempered, so she doesn't get easily angry.

straightforward

Max is straightforward when he talks about his opinion.

at first glance

At first glance she seemed a bit cold.

laid-back

He was laid-back about his tests, which I didn't understand at all.

a good sense of humor

I like men with a good sense of humor best.

conscientious

I look up to her as she does all her work in a conscientious manner.

🔍 주제: 장소묘사

industrialized

scenery
The scenery from the top of the mountain was magnificent.

along the riverside
I walk my dog along the riverside every morning.

gorgeous
The hotel room had a gorgeous view.

world famous
homelike atmosphere
It seemed that the company had a homelike atmosphere.

be well known for
The place is well known for its beautiful scenery.

metropolitan city

🔍 주제: 행동묘사

imitate
My son, j, likes imitating a superman.

hesitate
well spoken
My boss is smart, well spoken, and warm hearted.

carry out
In the project, I was asked to carry out a survey.

hang out with

I hang out with j on the weekends going fishing.

not to mention

get used to
I got used to getting up at 5 in the morning to go to work.

get an impression

come to a conclusion
The meeting lasted two hours, but it ended without coming to
a conclusion.

become familiar with

get together
Let's get together for a drink this Saturday.

flexible
to work flexible hours.
needless to say
Needless to say, the problem is the cost and time.

abuse one's power

Hotel Glossary

객실 부문

A

- Accommodation 관광 여행객이 여행 중 잠자리를 얻을 수 있는 총 숙박시설을 칭한다.

- Accordion door 호텔의 연회장이나 식당 등에서 고정된 문을 사용하는 것이 아니라, 자유롭게 이동이 가능하도록 한 칸막이 문 시스템을 만들어 설계되어진 문

- Adjoining rooms 객실과 객실이 인접해 있는 객실을 말한다(사이에 문이 없음). 일행이 여러 명이 있는 경우 동일한 층에 인접해서 객실을 배정한다.

- Advance deposit guarantee 손님이 도착하기 전 일정액을 예치하도록 하는 예약보증의 한 형태

- Amenity 추가요금 없이 고객의 안락함과 편의를 위해 객실에 비치하거나 고객에게 제공되는 품목

B

- Baggage 여행 시 소지하는 개인 소유물, 수하물

- Bath blankets 아주 큰 욕실용 타월, bath sheets라고도 한다.

- Bath tub 욕조

- Bell man 호텔의 프런트 부근에 있으며 고객이 등록을 필한 후 객실까지 고객의 짐을 들고 안내하는 역할을 맡은 호텔의 종사원으로 미국에서는

Bell-hop이라고 한다.

• **Block(ed)**   판촉이나 식음료 부서 등의 요구에 의해 객실들을 잡아 놓은 것을 말하며, 예약이 되어 있는 관광단체·국제회의참석자·VIP를 위해 사전에 객실을 지정해 놓은 경우를 말함.

C

• **Check-in**   투숙절차를 밟는 것

• **Check-out**   퇴숙절차를 밟는 것, 고객의 출숙과 회계정리를 포함한 제반절차 및 호텔에서 퇴숙하는 과정

• **Check-out time**   숙박객이 퇴숙 당일날 객실을 비워 주는 시간(통상 12시)

• **Commercial rate**   고정고객이나 단골고객을 위한 객실 특별할인율

• **Concierge**   front office와 front service의 업무를 좀 더 원활하게 하기 위하여 lobby에 상주하며, 고객의 편의도모를 위해 일하는 부서 또는 직원을 지칭하며, 고객의 rooming, telex, fax 전송, 항공권 예약, 고객 상담 등을 한다.

• **Connecting room**   2개의 객실이 연결된 객실을 말하며, 객실과 객실 사이에 통용문이 있는 객실이다. 객실과 객실 사이에 열쇠가 없이 드나들 수 있는 연쇄통용객실을 말한다.

• **Corporate guarantee**   상용 여행자의 No Show를 줄이기 위해 호텔과 그 보증인이 재정책임 여하를 계약상으로 협조, 동의한 예약 보증의 형태

D

• **Day rate**   적어도 overnight 이상 체재 시에 적용되는 객실 할인율

• **Day shift**   호텔 종업원의 근무시간으로서 보통 07:00~15:00까지를 말한다.

- **Day use** 대개 오전 11시부터 오후 6시까지 대실하는 것으로 정상요금의 50% 적용

- **Deposit reservation** 선불예약

- **DM(Direct Mail)** 호텔판촉 담당직원이 고객유치를 위해서 고객의 가정이나 거래처 및 회사·여행사·각종 사회단체 등에 발송

- **D.N.C.O.(did not check out)** 숙박하면서 발생시킨 비용은 정산하였으나 front office에는 알리지 않고 떠난 경우

- **DND(Do Not Disturb)** DND카드는 투숙객이 객실 내에서 중요한 회의를 하거나 수면 중일 때 방해하지 말라는 뜻으로 문고리에 걸어 놓는 카드이다.

- **Door knob** 호텔의 객실출입문에 걸어 놓는 인쇄된 안내문들의 일종인데 대부분이 Room Service 혹은 Housekeeping 부서에서 고객 서비스용으로 사용하는 것이다. 'DND'카드와 'Make up the Room'카드 등이 있다.

- **Door man** 현관 앞에 드나드는 차량에 대한 대리 Parking 업무와 자동차의 호출. check-in 하시는 고객의 영접 및 Goodbye 서비스를 행하는 호텔의 종사원

- **Double-locked** 고객이 객실부 서비스 받기를 원하지 않아 객실 안쪽 dead bolt로 객실을 잠궈 버린 상태로 일반적인 Pass Key로 열 수가 없다.

- **Double room** 2명이 이용하는 객실

- **Due out** 당일 체크아웃시간 이후 객실이 빈다는 것을 알리는 객실 상황표시 용어

E

- **Executive Floor** 상용고객을 위하여 세계적 수준의 최고급 서비스를 제공하는 객실층(귀빈층)

F

- FIT(Free Independent Traveller)   개인적으로 호텔에 숙박하는 고객

- Floor Master key   층의 객실을 열 수 있는 열쇠

- Folio   호텔 내 객실에 머물면서 사용한 비용명세서

- Front of the House   호텔 부서 중 고객과의 접촉이 많은 부서로 식음료나 객실 부서를 말한다.

- Front Office Clerk   고객을 Check-in시켜 드리고 전체적인 Room의 가능성 여부를 체크하는 사람

- Full House   전객실 판매를 말하며, 모든 객실이 다 판매되어 100% 판매율을 의미한다.

G

- Guaranteed Reservation   예약이 취소되지 않도록 고객이 얼마의 보증금을 내면 고객이 도착한 다음 날 체크아웃 시간까지 객실예약 상태가 유지되는 것

- Go show   빈자리(객실)를 기다리는 손님이나 공석을 기다리는 여객 Standby By Passenger를 말한다.

- Grand Master Key   객실 전체를 열 수 있는 열쇠를 말하며, 하나의 열쇠로서 모든 객실을 다 열 수 있으나, 안에서 잠근 것은 예외이다.

- Guest History(Card)   고객의 방문기록 카드로 지정된 객실료와 특별한 요구사항 및 신용능력평가를 기록하여 보다 나은 고객 서비스를 위해 보관한다.

H

- House Phone   호텔 로비에 있는 관내 전용 전화

- House use   호텔 직원이 무료로 객실을 이용하고 있음을 나타내는 객실상황
  표시

K

- Key Drop   객실열쇠를 퇴실 및 외출 시 열쇠투입구에 넣는 것

- Key Rack   객실열쇠를 보관하는 선반

L

- Late Arrival   호텔예약시간보다 늦게 도착하는 것

- Late check-out   호텔 정상 체크아웃 시간보다 늦게 체크아웃하는 것

- Log   업무일지로서 몇몇 영업부문에서 사용하는 업무활동 기록대장이다. 예를
  들면, 고객의 텔렉스 등 우편물 등을 이 대장에 기록하여 고객에게 전
  달할 때 서명을 받는다. 이를 로그북이라 한다.

- Lost and Found Office   분실물계

M

- Make Bed   사용한 베드의 시트를 갈아 끼우고 새로 베드를 만드는 것을 말한다.

- Make-up   객실 청소를 총칭하며 말함. 고객이 등록되어 있는 상태에서 침대의
  린넨류를 갈고, 객실, 화장실 등을 청소하는 것

- Master key   이중 잠금 장치가 된 객실을 제외한 전 객실을 열 수 있는 열쇠

N

• **No Show**   예약을 해놓고 아무 연락 없이 나타나지 않는 고객

O

• **Occupancy Rate**   호텔객실이용률, 항공기의 좌석이용률

• **Occupied**   고객이 객실을 현재 사용 중임을 나타냄

• **On Change** 객실정돈 중이라는 표시로서, 고객이 객실에서 퇴실하고 난 뒤 아직 청소가 완료되지 않는 상태

• **O.O.O(Out of order)**   수리, 청소 등으로 인해 판매될 수 없는 객실

• **Out of order**   객실을 보수 중이거나 대청소, 재배치 등의 이유로 고객에게 판매가 불가능한 객실

• **Out of Town**   객실 투숙 중 타 지역으로 출장 간 손님의 객실

R

• **Rack**   랙이라 하며, Room Rack과 동의어임

• **Rack Rate**   정가 객실요금, 호텔에서 공시한 객실요금으로 경영진에 의해 정해진 객실의 최고가격(할인되지 않은 상태의 가격)

• **Room Inspection**   객실 청결도와 유지 상태를 조직적으로 점검하는 세부과정

• **Room Rack**   객실상황을 포괄하는 것

• **Room service**   호텔 객실의 고객요청으로 음료, 식사 등을 보내주는 담당 계 또는 호텔의 객실에서 하는 식사를 말한다.

S

- Single Room   한 명이 이용하는 객실

- Skipper   정당한 퇴실 절차를 이행하지 않고 떠나는 고객, 객실료를 안내고 도
  망간 고객이며, 식당에서 식대 등을 지불하지 않고 도주해 버리는 고객

- Sleep Out   외박고객을 말하며, 객실료를 지불했으나 등록한 객실에서 숙박하
  지 않고 외부에서 숙박한 고객을 말한다.

- Sleeper   사무착오로 인하여 Room Rack에 투숙 중으로 되어 있는 빈 방을 말한다.

T

- Tariff   요금표

V

- Valet Parking   고객의 차를 호텔의 종업원이 직접 운전하여 전용 주차장에
  주차해 주는 서비스

W

- Walk in Guest   예약 없이 찾아오는 고객

◀ 식음료 부문 ▶

A

- Abbreviation 종사원, 수납원, 주방과의 미리 약속된 약어식 표현

- A'Card 현금지불보고서 카드

- After Dinner Cart 여러 종류의 Brandy 및 Liqueur를 진열하여 고객이 신택하여 마실 수 있도록 만들어 보편적으로 고급식당에서 사용하는 이동식 수레

- A la ~ 풍의, ~식의, ~을 곁들인

- A La Carte 일품요리(메뉴 중 자기가 좋아하는 요리를 선택하여 주문하는 형식)

- A La Mode 각종 파이류에 아이스크림을 얹어서 제공하는 일종의 후식

- American Breakfast 감자를 곁들인 달걀요리와 주스·토스트·커피가 제공되며, 베이컨·햄·소시지 등을 선택하여 먹는 아침식사

- Aperitif 식전에 식욕을 증진시키기 위해서 마시는 술로서 각종 칵테일 및 Aperitif Wine이 있다.

B

- Baked Alaska Meringue(설탕·달걀흰자 등으로 만든)로 덮어 입힌 케이크나 아이스크림을 Brandy 같은 알코올을 뿌려 불을 붙여 갈색이 되면 즉석에서 고객에게 서비스하는 것

- Bar 주류를 위주로 하여 영업하는 장소

- Bar Charge 바(bar) 부문의 판매거래에서 발생한 수익의 합계

- Bartender 칵테일 조주를 위시하여 주류 전반에 대한 서비스를 담당하는 사람

- Base 칵테일을 만들 때 가장 많이 함유되는 술을 뜻한다.

- Basils   향료의 일종

- Blanc   흰색 또는 맑은 것을 의미한다. Vin Blanc은 백포도주, White sauce, 백색의 린넨, 달걀의 흰자위, 화이트 미트를 의미한다.

- Blend   두 가지 이상의 재료를 혼합, 즉 블랜디드 위스키(blended whisky)라 하면, 몰트 위스키(malt whisky)와 그래인 위스키(grain whisky)의 두 가지를 혼합한 위스키를 말한다.

- Boiled Eggs   삶은 달걀

- Bread Basket   빵 담는 바구니

- Brunch   아침과 점심 사이에 하는 식사를 말한다. 아침(breakfast)과 점심(Lunch)의 합성어. 주로 10~12시 사이에 간단한 음식으로 제공된다.

C

- Call Liquor   고객에 의해서 요청된 특별한 상표의 주류

- Camembert Cheese   Soft Cheese의 일종으로 프랑스 Normandy 지방의 Vimoutiers 근교 Camembert(까망베르) 마을에서 처음 만들어졌다. 먹을 때 외피를 벗겨 먹는 것이 보통인데, 이것은 자극적인 냄새가 너무 강하고, 과숙한 경우에는 Ammonia 냄새도 나기 때문이다.

- Canape   빵을 잘게 여러 가지 모양으로 만들어 그 위에 각종 가공된 음식물을 얹어서 한입에 먹을 수 있게 만든 요리

- Carafe   하우스 와인을 담아서 제공하는 Decanter

- Carfe   요금표(메뉴)

- Carte de Jeur   그날의 특별메뉴(daily special menu)

- Captain   업장에서 웨이터나 웨이트리스들을 통솔하며, 어떤 한 section을 담당하여 주문을 받는 주임급 직원

- **Caster Set**   테이블에 놓는 소금과 후추 세트를 지칭한다.

- **Catering**   식음료부서에 속하면서 일종의 출장요리

- **Caviar**   철갑상어(sturgeon)의 알

- **Chateau Briand**   소의 등뼈 양쪽에 붙어 있는 가장 연한 안심의 머리부분을 말한다.

- **Chef**   식당의 주방장(kitchen chief)

- **Chilled Water**   식당에서 고객의 Water Glass에 따라 주는 냉수(ice water)

- **Chinaware**   각종 도자기 집기류

- **Cocktail Lounge**   라운지(lounge) 옆에 바(bar)를 설비하여 양주에서 소프트 드링크까지 이른바 음료를 마시면서 담화하는 넓고 큰 방을 칵테일 라운지라고 한다.

- **Continental Breakfast**   Juice, Toasgt, Roll or Sweet Roll, Coffee(tea or milk)로 구성된 아침식사, 메뉴에 달걀을 곁들이지 않은 조식. 음료(커피·홍차·주스·코코아·밀크)와 빵과 Butter(jam)만의 식사

- **Continental Plan**   유럽식 아침식사로 보통 커피 또는 우유와 빵·치즈를 제공

- **Corkage**   손님이 가져온 술병에 대한 서비스 룰(마개를 뽑아주는 서비스 룰)

- **Corkage Charge**   호텔 식당에 있어서 그 식당의 술을 구매하지 않고 고객이 가지고 온 술을 마실 때 마개를 뽑아 주는 봉사료

- **Covers**   업장에서 음료와 음식을 시키는 고객의 수

- **Crepe Suzette**   얇게 구워낸 팬케이크로 맛이 좋은 시럽 소스와 서브되는 둥글게 말아서 만든 것. 보통 술을 약간 넣어 데워서 Brown 색깔로 만든다.

- **Crib**   어린이를 위한 유아용 침대로 고객의 요청에 따라 추가되며, Baby Bed라고도 한다.

- Cuisine   요리 혹은 조리법

- Cutlet   얇게 저민 고기나 생선에 밀가루·달걀·빵가루 등을 묻혀서 Fried한 요리

D

- Daily Menu   식당의 전략메뉴라 할 수 있는 이 식단은 매일 시장에서 나오는 특별재료를 구입하여 조리장의 기술을 최대로 발휘하여 고객의 식욕을 자극할 수 있는 메뉴이다.

- Daily Special Menu   주방장이 제공하는 그날의 특별메뉴

- Danish Blue   덴마크산 푸른곰팡이 치즈

- Danish Pastry   덴마크식 빵으로 반죽을 유지로 싸서 퍼프 페이스트리(puff pastry)처럼 밀고 접기를 반복하여 굽는 빵

- Decanter   각종 음료를 담는 용기로서 Cocktail Decanter, Wine Decanter가 있다.

- Dessert wine   주(main)식사가 끝나고 디저트(dessert)를 먹을 때 같이 먹는 와인(wine)으로서 주로 Sweet Sherry Wine, Sweet Red Wine, Sweet White Wine 등이 Dessert Wine으로 많이 애용된다.

- Dissert   식후에 먹는 음식으로서 Main Course를 먹고 나면 Dessert를 제공한다. 주로 Sweet와 Savoury 및 Fruit의 3가지 요소가 포함된 것을 제공

- Door Knob Menu   객실에 비치된 것으로 손님께서 원하는 날짜·시간·물품을 표기하여 당일 2:00까지 Door Knob에 걸어 놓으면, 이를 룸 서비스 직원이 수거하여 Order Taker가 시간별로 분류하여 Bill을 작성

- Draft Beer   제조과정에서 발효균을 살균하지 않은 생맥주(lager beer)

- Dressed Food   음식상품으로서의 가치를 높이기 위하여 드레서(dresser)에 의해 예쁘게 장식되고 정리된 음식

- Dry   주조상의 용어로 드라이라고 할 때는 당분이 없다는 뜻이며, Dry Wine이

라고 할 때는 단맛이 없는 포도주를 의미

- Dutch Coffee　물을 사용하여 3시간 이상 추출한 독특하고 향기 좋은 커피

E

- Entree　정식의 여러 코스 중 중심이 되는 요리로, 쇠고기·송아지고기·돼지 고기·양고기뿐만 아니라 생선이나 조류 종류도 식사 코스의 중심이 된다면 앙트레로 조리할 수 있다.

- Espresso　이탈리아식 커피추출법으로 농도를 진하게 추출해내는 방법이다.

- Executive Chef　모든 주방장(chef)을 지휘·통솔하는 주방부장으로 실제적인 조리 (cooking)보다는 메뉴계획이라든가 인사 등 주방부서의 행정적인 면을 담당

F

- F&B(Food & Beverage)　식료·음료를 통칭하는 말

- Filet　육류나 생선의 뼈나 지방질을 추려낸 상태

- Flat Ware　테이블에 쓰이는 은기물류의 총칭(cutlery)

- Fried Eggs(turn over, sunny side up)　프라이 에그(양면 구운, 한 면만 구운)

G

- Garde Manger　찬 음식을 다루는 부서 또는 그 부서의 관리자

- Garnish　먹을 수 있는 재료로 음식물을 보기 좋게 장식해 놓은 Dish(예: Caviar)

- Gouda Cheese　네덜란드 남부에 위치한 가우다 근교에서 200여 년 전부터 만 들어진 것으로 Edam Cheese와 유사하나 지방함량이 높으며, 외피는 적 색으로 염색한다. 이 치즈는 살균시키지 않은 우유를 가지고 만든

Sweet Curd Cheese로서 Semi-Soft에서 Hard Cheese까지 다양하다.

- Great Wine   포도주를 만들어서 15년 이상 저장하여 50년 이내에 마시는 와인을 말한다.

- Gueridon   프렌치 서비스에 사용하는 작은 식요리대

- Gueridon Service   식당 서비스 중 게리동을 사용한 서비스를 뜻한다. 게리동이란 프렌치 서비스와 같은 정교한 식당 서비스를 위해 사용되는 바퀴가 달린 사이드 테이블

H

- Hard Boiled Eggs   완숙

- Hothouse   생후 8~15주 정도 된 어린 양

- Housewine   호텔이 영업신장을 위하여 정한 기획와인으로 대체적으로 저렴한 상품을 Glass단위로 판매할 수 있는 와인

L

- La Newburg   달걀노른자 · 크림 · 와인 등으로 만든 Sauce

- Lager Beer   제조과정에서 발효균을 살균하여 병에 넣은 맥주를 말한다.

- Lounge   의자 · 테이블 등을 비치하고 있는 장소로 스페이스가 더 넓은 것은 로비(lobby)라고 한다.

- Luggage Chair   고객의 짐을 놓을 수 있게 만든 의자

- Luncheon   오찬을 뜻하며, 아침과 저녁 중간에 먹는 가벼운 식사를 말한다. 대개 3~4 코스로 구성되어 있다. 즉 수프(soup), 앙뜨레(entree), 후식(dessert), 음료(coffee or tea)로 구분

M

- Main Dining Room 주식당

- Main Dining Seruice 호텔의 부대시설인 식당 중에서 그 호텔의 정식식당으로 식사와 오락을 함께 즐길 수 있는 풀 코스(full course)에 가장 적합하며, 메인 다이닝에 들어갈 때는 넥타이를 매는 것이 에티켓이다.

- Maroilles 프랑스산 연질 치즈

- Midium 중간으로 익힌 요리, 알맞게 익힌 요리

- Midium Rare Rare보다는 좀 더 익히며, Medium보다는 좀 덜 익힌 것으로, 역시 자르면 피가 보이도록 하여야 한다. 조리시간은 약 3~4분 정도이고, 고기 내부의 온도는 55℃ 정도이다.

- Menu Tent Card 천막식으로 접어서 식탁에 세워 놓은 메뉴카드

- Mignon 쇠고기의 안심 끝부분을 스테이크용으로 토막 내서 베이컨을 감은 것(예: filet mignon)

O

- Order Slip 웨이터가 작성하는 식음료의 주문전표

- Order Taker 식당이나 룸 서비스에 있어서 주문을 받는 사람

- Over Easy 달걀 한쪽이 살짝 익으면 엎어서 다른 한쪽을 익혀 양쪽의 흰자만 약간 익힌 것

- Over Hard 달걀요리의 일종인 Fried Egg의 요리방법으로 흰자와 노른자를 모두 익힌 것

- Over Heat 석쇠 위에 고기를 얹어 직접 열을 받게 하여 뒤집어 가며 굽는 조리법

- Over Medium Fried Egg의 요리방법으로 흰자는 완전히 익고, 노른자는 약간 익힌 것

P

- Plate Service 식당 서비스 중 가장 간단하고 빠른 서비스방법으로 주방에서 음식을 미리 접시(plate)에 담아 놓은 것을 접객원들이 날라다가 서브하는 형식으로 비교적 숙련된 종사원을 필요로 하지 않기 때문에 대중식당에서 많이 이용

R

- Rare 육류를 요리할 때 색상과 촉감으로써 그 익은 정도를 나타내는 용어의 하나로서 완전 날고기를 따뜻하게 데운 정도를 표시하는 용어
- Room Service 객실에 투숙 중인 고객의 편의를 위해 식사 · 음료 등을 객실에 운반하는 서비스를 행하거나 영업과 관련된 고객의 요청사항을 대행하는 호텔식음부의 영업부서
- Russian Service 육류의 통구이나 통생선 혹은 날 종류의 통구이로 고객들이 볼 수 있는 옆 테이블에 보이게 차려 놓고 고객으로 하여금 스스로 자기 몫을 자르도록 유도하는 러시아 사람들의 옛 관습에서 기인된 형태의 서비스로 주 음식접시를 놓고 고객들이 스스로 들 수 있도록 접시를 돌리는 형식

S

- Scrambled Eggs 풀어 볶은 달걀(달걀 2개 반+우유 큰 스푼을 섞어 저은 후 미리 버터를 녹여 놓은 프라이팬에 붓고 약한 불로 저어 만든 달걀요리)
- Snack Bar 흔히 서서 식사를 하는 간이식당. Counter Service와 Self Service 형식으로 제공

- **Sunny Side Up**   달걀을 한 면만 익힌 후 살라맨더(salamander)에 잠시 넣어서 윗면을 덥혀서 요리

T

- **Table D'Hote**   정식(행사주관자인 host의 의견에 따라 정해진 코스대로 진행되는 음식)

- **Turned Over**   Fried Egg의 요리방법 중의 하나로, 턴드 오버에는 오버 이지(over easy), 오버 미디엄(over medium), 오버 하드(over hard) 등이 있다.

W

- **Wagon Service**   요리의 서비스방식으로 작은 차가 달린 왜건에 요리를 싣고 서비스를 행한다. 경우에 따라서는 고객 앞에서 간단한 요리를 행할 수도 있다.

- **Well-Done**   많이 익힌 스테이크요리

 Answer Key

• • • **Quiz**

Chapter 1.

1. My friend works as an English instructor.

2. I live in a villa.

3. People walk along the lake.

4. It happened one year ago.

Chapter 2.

1. My apartment complex is boring.

2. While watching the TV, I felt sad.

3. I became comfortable.

4. He was a little nervous.

Chapter 3.

1. I play baseball with my friend.

2. I have a notebook computer.

3. I use a vacuum cleaner to sweep the floor.

4. I like Jazz music.

Chapter 4.

1. He showed us how to play soccer.

2. I bought my teacher some gifts.

3. My friend taught me how to use the smart phone.

4. My friend gave me a book.

Chapter 5.

1. I helped my mother clean

2. Going to the hospital makes me feel nervous.

3. It made the living room brighter

4. She helped her team win the championship.

Chapter 6.

1. There is a bookstore on the campus

2. There are many buildings in my neighborhood.

3. There are many books and clothes in my room.

4. There are a lot of tourist attractions in Seoul.

Chapter 7.

1. My office is quiet, so it is easy to rest during my coffee break.

2. It is my job to conduct orientation seminars for employees.

3. It is important to wear the right type of footwear to prevent injuries.

4. It is difficult to spend time together when we are working.

Chapter 8.

1. He can play many different characters.

2. My home is very large, so I can keep many things in it.

3. I pack a smart phone so that I can contact the people I will meet.

4. I asked hotel concierge if they could change my flight.

Chapter 9.

1. I Want to work for a hotel in the future.

2. I have worked at Global Hotel for three years.

3. I like to make fried rice on Sunday afternoon.

4. He took a lot of pictures during the trip.

Chapter 10.

1. There are many buildings on the campus.

2. I have a bed, a desk, and a chair in the room.

3. We usually prepare dinner together at home.

4. I usually listen to music on the subway.

Chapter 11.

1. It was memorable because I launched a new product.

2. I get distracted if other people are around.

3. When I watch a horror movie, I scream loudly.

4. Before I cook, I usually prepare the ingredients.

Chapter 12.

1. The problem was that I overcooked the noodles.

2. I asked the airline staff if they could change my flight.

3. The biggest change in TV program is that there are many reality shows now.

4. My boss announced that we would have a special guest.

Chapter 13.

1. Can you help me find cheese.

   Could you help me find cheese.

2. Do you have other types of cheese?

3. Can I reserve a table for 10 people?

   Could I reserve a table for 10 people?

4. Do you know if I can still enroll?

●●● **Practical Point**

Chapter 1.

1. G Yes, I am. Do you have parking?

    R Yes, we have (parking) available in the basement.

       Our guests can use it anytime.

2. R Thank you, sir. When would you like to (stay) with us?

    G The ninth of December.

Chapter 2.

1. O Ms, we are sorry but the line seems to be (busy) at the moment.

    G Very well, I'll call back later.

2. G Is there any (cancellation charge)?

    R No. Our cancellation policy is twenty-four hours prior to the arrival.

Chapter 3.

1. G Yes, her name is Powell.

    O I beg your (pardon)?

2. O Excuse me, but I'm afraid there is no Hungarian speaking staff (available).

       Do you speak English or Korean?

    G Nem... koszonom szepen (hung up)

Chapter 4.

1. G How can I get to Incheon Airport?

    C There is a (limousine) bus and taxis. Also, we can arrange a car with driver.

2. G I'd like to buy some Korean (souveniors) for my wife.

    C What kind of items are you looking for?

3. C We recommend Gyeongbokgung Palace and Deoksugung Palace for a one
       day (sightseeing trip).

       Both are one of Korea's representative palaces in Seoul, famous for its
       magnificent structure and unique beauty.

    G I've heard of both of them.

       Will it be most convenient to travel by taxi?

Chapter 5.

   1. G My room is on the top floor, isn't it?

            It must have a beautiful (view).

            It's so exciting.

       B You can see Mt. Bugak very clearly today.

   2. G Yes. Thanks.

            Which (floor) is my room on?

       B Your room is on the thirty-fourth floor in the Main Building, Mr. Ford.

Chapter 6.

   1. D I will keep your luggage in the (cloakroom) by the main entrance.

            Please be ready to board the bus 10 minutes before departure time.

       G Thanks.

   2. B You have two pieces of (luggage). Is that correct, sir?

       G That's correct.

Chapter 7.

   1. G₁ Yes, I had two cans of beer and that's it.

          (to G₂) And you?

       G₂ Well, I had a can of orange juice and a small bottle of brandy from the

          (mini-bar)

   2. G Thank you.

       R You're welcome.

           Our bellman will (guide) you to your room.

           Have a pleasant stay, sir.

   3. R (Could) you fill out this form, please?

       G Certainly.

Chapter 8.

   1. G₁ Thank you, it was such a wonderful stay!

       G₂ Yes, we really enjoyed our stay.

          We're so sure that we'll be back again for our next (visit)!

   2. R Here you are. (May) I have your signature, please?

     G Certainly.

Chapter 9.

1. H Here you are, sir.

        You requested we remove this (stain), Unfortunately we couldn't.

        Our supervisor tried to remove it by using a special method.

        We are very sorry.

     G Oh, no! Is there another way?

2. H Good morning, Mr. Oliveila. This is Housekeeping.

        I'm here to pick up your (laundry).

     G Ah, you came so quickly. It's not really yet.

Chapter 10.

1. R May I have your (signature) on the bill?

     G Sure. Here you are.

2. R Your order, please.

     G Yes, I'd like to have an (American breakfast).

        I'd like to have a glass of orange juice, scrambled eggs with bacon, two

        pieces of toast and decaffeinated coffee, if you have it.

3. R Yes, breakfast at seven o'clock for Mr. Bob Plant, (room number) seventy

        eighteen?

     G No, one-seven-one-eight!

Chapter 11.

1. G I don't have much time. I just want a (quick) meal.

        Can you recommend anything simple on the menu?

     W I would like to recommend pasta.

2. G Yes, I am. But unfortunately, I don't know what he/she looks like.

        Could you help me find him/her?

     W Certainly, sir/madam. Could you please write down the (person's name)

        on the memo pad?

        I will check for you.

3. W May I have your name, please?

(What name did you make the reservation under?)

G   Kim Myunghak. I reserved a (table) for three.

Chapter 12.

1. W   Certainly, sir/madam. Did you enjoy your meal?

        Would you like to pay by cash or by credit card?

    G   I would like to (charge) it to my room.

        Is it possible to charge here?

2. G   I ordered the American breakfast but as you can see, I have been served the

        continental breakfast.

    W   I'm sorry, sir/madam. I'll bring your (order) immediately.

        Could you wait just a moment?

Chapter 13.

1. G   Could I see the bill? I think you've overcharged me.

        We only had 3 (portions)

    W   Oh, I'm very sorry for the mistake, sir/madam.

2. G   Where can I buy some (groceries)?

    W   The building right nest to the hotel is the department store.

        You can buy some groceries over there.

●●● **Activity (Making dialogue)**

Chapter 14.

Topic 1. **Reservation Service (객실예약의 서비스)**

Conversation 1 : I'd like to change my reservation...

G   I'd like to change my reservation.

R   Certainly, sir.

First, may I have your name please, sir?

G   My name is George Green.

R   Thank you very much, Mr. Green.

How may I help you?

G   I'd like to change my arrival date from the fifteenth to the seventeenth of May.

R   Certainly. You will be arriving on the seventeenth of May and departing on the twentieth of May as in the original reservation, is this correct?

G   That's correct.

R   I will change our reservation starting from the seventeenth of May for three nights.

Topic 2. **Operator's Service (교환원의 서비스)**

Conversation 2 : Thank you for calling the Lotte Global Hotel.

O   Thank you for calling the Global Hotel.

This is Lee speaking. May I help you?

G   Hi, I'd like to make a Reservations.

O   Yes, sir.

I will connect you to Reservations.

One moment, please.

G   Thank you.

O   You're welcome.

Topic 3. **Concierge Service (컨시어지 서비스)**

Conversation 3 : We recommend Gyeongbokgung Palace and Deoksugung Palace

C   We recommend Gyeongbokgung Palace and Deoksugung Palace for a one day sightseeing trip.

Both are one of Korea's representative palaces in Seoul, famous for its magnificent structure and unique beauty.

G   I've heard of both of them.

Will it be most convenient to travel by taxi?

C   Yes, we suggest that you take the taxi for Gyeongbokgung Palace.

You can walk for Deoksugung Palace, which takes only 10 minutes.

Have a pleasant day, madam/sir.

Topic 4. **Door man/Bell man Service (도어맨/벨맨 서비스)**

Conversation 4 : I will show you to your room

B   I will show you to your room, Mr. Ford.

Elevators are on your right.

This way, please.

G   Yes. Thanks.

Which floor is my room on?

B   Your room is on the thirty-fourth floor in the Main Building, Mr. Ford.

G   How many stories does this hotel have?

B   Our hotel is thirty-eight stories high, and guest rooms are located between the seventh and the thirty-fourth floor.

G   My room is on the top floor, isn't it?

It must have a beautiful view.

It's so exciting.

B   You can see Mt. Bugak very clearly today

Chapter 15.

Topic 1 : **Front Service (프런트 서비스)**

Conversation 1 : Welcome

R   Welcome to the Global Hotel. May I help you?

G   Yes, my name is Schmidt, Arthur Schmidt.

And I booked a double room for four nights.

R   Yes, Mr. Schmidt, you booked a non-smoking double room for four nights and you are planning to check out on Wednesday?

G   Yes.

R   Could you fill out this form, please?

G   Certainly.

Topic 2. **Housekeeping Service**

Conversation 2 : I'm here to pick up your laundry.

H   Good morning, Mr. Smith. This is housekeeping.

     I'm here to pick up your laundry.

G   Ah, you came so quickly. It's not really yet.

H   No problem, sir. I will wait.

G   It's ready now. Here is everything.

H   (look inside of the laundry bag and check the sheet) Certainly, sir.

     We will have these back by five o'clock this afternoon.

G   I'm going out right now. I'd like you to deliver them to my room.

H   Certainly, sir.

     Shall we hang them up inside the closet?

G   Yes, that's a good idea. Thanks.

Topic 3. **Room Service**

Conversation 3 : Thank you for waiting, your breakfast is ready.

R   (Knock on the door)

G   Who is it?

R   This is room service.

     Thank you for waiting, your breakfast is ready.

G   (open the door) Come in.

R   Thank you, madam.

     Where would you like your breakfast?

G   Here, by the bed, please.

R   Certainly, a glass of apple juice, scrambled eggs with bacon, croissant and coffee, is this correct?

G   Yes, perfect.

R   Thank you very much.

Topic 4. **Food and Beverages Service**

Conversation 4 : I'll bring your order immediately.

G   Excuse me, this is not what I ordered.

W   Oh, really? I'm truly sorry.

      What did you order, sir/madam?

G   I ordered the American breakfast but as you can see, I have been served the continental breakfast.

W   I'm sorry, sir/madam. I'll bring your order immediately.

      Could you wait just a moment?

G   Okay.

●●● Reading Comprehension

Chapter 1.

    1. Q How many guests will there be?

        A There will be just one.

    2. Q What is James's telephone number?

        A Telephone number is 02-314-5768.

Chapter 2.

    1. Q How kinds of room does Mr. trump make reservation?

        A He make reservation a standard double room.

    2. Q When does Mr.Green want to make reservation?

        A He wants to make reservation on the Seventeenth of May.

Chapter 3.

    1. Q What is the name of the Hotel?

        A The name of the Hotel is Global Hotel.

    2. Q Has She connected to Domestic call?

        A Yes, She has connected to Domestic call.

    3. Q Where does the guest call to?

        A The guest calls to San Francisco.

Chapter 4.

    1. Q How long does it take to Yeoui-do?

        A It takes approximately thirty minutes.

    2. Q Does the guest want to join an organized tour?

        A No, she doesn't want to join an organized tour.

Chapter 5.

    1. Q What is Mr. Ford's room number?

        A He's room nember is two-one-o-one.

Chapter 6.

    1. Q Has Mr.Ford's wife arrived the Bell desk?

       A No, She hasn't arrived.

Chapter 7.

    1. Q Which floor is the guest going to stay?

       A He is going to stay on the twenty-eight floor of New wing.

Chapter 8.

    1. Q When did the Guest make thirty copies?

       A He made thirty copies Half an hour ago.

    2. Q Does Mrs. Wong paid by cash?

       A Yes, She paid by cash.

    3. Q Where does the clerk work?

       A The clerk works at Front desk.

Chapter 9.

    1. Q Where is Mr. Brown going to working?

       A He'll be working at the Business center.

    2. Q What does Mr. Brown order for the turndown service?

       A He ordered a couple of bottles of Mineral water.

Chapter 10.

    1. Q What does the guest order as a breakfast?

       A She orders a glass of apple juice, scrambled eggs with bacon, croissant and coffee.

Chapter 11.

    1. Q What does waiter advise to the guest?

       A We do have desinated smoking areas.

Chapter 12.

    1.   Q   How long would it take a quick meal?

        A   It will take about 15minutes.

    2.   Q   What does the guest order?

        A   He order the American breakfast.

Chapter 13.

    1.   Q   What is the guest's lost and found at the restaurant?

        A   They were black sunglasses with yellow frames.

•••• OPIc Answer

01. 자기 소개하기 [Self Introduction]

Q. Let's start the interview now. Tell me a little about yourself.

02. 가장 좋아하는 장소 묘사하기

Q1. You indicated in the survey that you like to go to the park. Describe your favorite park as much detail as possible. What make it so special?

Q2. Describe one of the movie theaters that you often go to. Where is it? Why do you choose to go there over many others?

03. 자전거 묘사하기

Q1. Can you tell me about your bicycle? What does it look like? Where did you bike it? Please describe your bicycle in as much as possible.

Q2. Let's talk about your bicycle routine. What kind of things do you do before and after riding a bicycle? Tell me about your typical bicycle routine from the beginning to the end.

Q3. When and how were you interested in riding a bicycle? Was there any special reason? How did you learn to ride it? Who taught you? Discuss your memorable experience in as much detail as you can.

04. Role-play Type 1. 질문하기 정보요청 – 초대 약속관련 핵심패턴

Q1. Let me give a situation for you to act out. A friend wants to go jogging with you. Call your friend to go jogging. Ask him or her 3 or 4 questions about jogging.

Q2. Let me give a situation for you to act out. You just moved into a new house and want to purchase new furniture. Call a furniture store and ask three or four questions about the furniture you want to buy.

04. Role-play Type 2. 상황대처하기

Q1. Let me give a situation for you to act out. You are supposes to go to the park with your friend but you can't. Call your friend to explain the situation. Give 3 or 4 Suggestions.

Q2. Upon arriving at the theater, you realized that you have ticket for the wrong movie. Explain your situation to the ticket seller and thenmake 2 or 3 suggestion that will help you resolve your problem.

05. 은행에서 계좌 오픈하는 방법 말하기

Q. Now tell me about the process of opening a new bank account. Describe the whole procedure starting with when you first step into the bank.

06. 재활용하는 방법 말하기

Q. Tell me about the recycling program in your country. How do people recycle waste materials?

07. 이슈 이야기하기

Q1. Nowadays, people travel more than ever. Tell me about some issues people are interested in and care about most.

Q2. Tell me about the issues about housing in your country. What issues are told in broadcasting and news?

08. 가장 좋아하는 장소 비교하기

Q. Please compare the movie theaters you often go to. How has the places changed over the years?

저 자 소 개

백지은

- 현, 세종대학교 미래교육원 호텔경영학과 교수
  세종대학교, 신한대학교, 백석대학교 교수
  삼성전자 임원강사
  세종대학교 호텔관광경영대학원 호텔관광경영학 석사
  미국 UC Berkeley Extension 경영 수료
  세종대학교 호텔관광경영학 경영학사
  롯데호텔시울잠실 Guest Relations Officer

[저서]
Hotel Restaurant Service English(호텔외식실무영어)

김은숙

- 현, 세종대학교 미래교육원 호텔경영학과 교수
  세종대학교 미래교육원 외식경영학과 교수
  서울여자대학교 대학원 경영학 박사
  한양대학교 경영대학원 경영학 석사
  세종대학교 호텔경영학과 경영학사
  한양여자대학교, 삼육대학교, 서울여자대학교 교수

[저서]
현대서비스운영관리, 서비스경영론, 관광사업론, 품질경영
서비스경영, 호텔경영론, 신품질경영, 경영학원론
최신 외식산업의 창업 및 경영 등

한국외식산업학회 부회장
한국호텔관광학회 이사

저자와의
합의하에
인지첩부
생략

Practical Hotel Service English (호텔실무영어)

2017년 3월 15일 초 판 1쇄 발행
2024년 1월 30일 제3판 3쇄 발행

지은이 백지은 · 김은숙
펴낸이 진욱상
펴낸곳 백산출판사
교 정 편집부
본문디자인 오행복
표지디자인 오정은

등 록 1974년 1월 9일 제406-1974-000001호
주 소 경기도 파주시 회동길 370(백산빌딩 3층)
전 화 02-914-1621(代)
팩 스 031-955-9911
이메일 edit@ibaeksan.kr
홈페이지 www.ibaeksan.kr

ISBN 979-11-5763-252-7 93740
값 18,500원